VIDEO ART

Institute of Contemporary Art
University of Pennsylvania
Philadelphia, Pennsylvania

January 17 to February 28, 1975

The Contemporary Arts Center
Cincinnati, Ohio
March 22 to May 30, 1975

Museum of Contemporary Art
Chicago, Illinois
June 28 to August 31, 1975

Wadsworth Atheneum
Hartford, Connecticut
PARTICIPANTS   September 17 to November 2, 1975

The exhibition and publication are partially supported by the
National Endowment for the Arts, a federal agency, with
assistance from the Commonwealth of Pennsylvania Council
on the Arts, and The Philadelphia Foundation.

TABLE OF CONTENTS

ACKNOWLEDGMENTS

In 1973 VIDEO ART was a mere idea; it was an intention to survey the growing use of video by artists in the United States and abroad. From the very beginning Jack Boulton, director of The Contemporary Arts Center in Cincinnati, shared my enthusiasm for the undertaking; in fact, his encouragement and the Center's early commitment to participate in this project, followed by the interest of Stephen Prokopoff, director of the Museum of Contemporary Art in Chicago, made this exhibition and publication feasible for all three institutions.

The development of the exhibition owes much to the generous assistance and advice of many. I am deeply indebted to Robert Stearns, director of The Kitchen in New York, for invaluable information, practical suggestions and inspiration during the exhibition's early planning stages. The project's focus was greatly clarified by discussions with Jack Boulton, Eugene Feldman, Christopher Speeth and Patricia Stewart. They generously shared their insights about video with me as did the many artists I visited during my research travels. My perspective on video art was sharpened by conversations with persons from broadcast television, notably Fred Barzyk, director of the Television Workshop at WGBH-TV in Boston and Carol Brandenburg, Peter Crown and David Silver from the Television Laboratory at WNET-TV in New York. At CBS-TV in New York, Merle Brockway, director of Camera Three, and Louis Dorfsman, Vice President of Advertising and Design, provided valuable insights and advice about the relation of video to network television.

David A. Ross, deputy director of the Long Beach Museum of Art in Long Beach, California, kindly made his research material available, for which we are most grateful. George Bolling, video curator at the de Saisset Art Gallery and Museum at the University of Santa Clara, and Jane Livingston, curator at the Los Angeles County Museum of Art, were resources for video activities in California which greatly enriched my research trip to the west coast. Peggy Gayle of The Canada Council in Ottawa and Elke Hayden from A Space in Toronto were extremely helpful in expanding my knowledge of video activities in Canada. In arranging for videotapes by European artists, I was helped by Barbara London, curatorial assistant at The Museum of Modern Art in New York, and by Anna Canepa; both freely shared their knowledge of European material with me. Irene von Zahn from René Block Gallery Ltd. in New York as well as René Block in Berlin graciously assisted with the transportation of videotapes from West Germany. William Viola from Art/Tapes/22 in Florence arranged for the delivery of tapes from Italy with cheerful efficiency. Fujiko Nakaya at Video Hiroba in Tokyo coordinated communications with artists from Japan. I am deeply indebted to Antonio H. Amaral, Aracy A. Amaral, Luis Camnitzer, Regina Cornwell and Luis Villares for information about the use of video by artists in Brazil. Above all, I extend my thanks to Walter Zanini, director of the Museum of Contemporary Art at the University of São Paulo, for sending us the Brazilian tapes which are included in the exhibition. I also wish to extend special thanks to Michael Demetriades, film editor at Clio, not only for spending endless hours showing me old TV commercials, but for editing the selections made for this exhibition.

Warm thanks to Anna Canepa, The Videotape Distribution, Inc., to Joyce Nevreaux, Castelli-Sonnabend Tapes and Films, Inc., to Michael Tims at Art Metropole and to Howard Wise as well as Flora Meyer and John Trayna at Electronic Arts Intermix, Inc. All extended kindness to me during my many hours previewing materials for the exhibition.

The installation of an exhibition of video works cannot be separated from electronic technology. For the Institute's staff, the presentation of works that is electronic, audio, visual and temporal was an uncharted challenge. The development and realization of the exhibition come from the absolute devotion and tireless efforts of the Institute's staff. I am exceedingly grateful to Michael A. Quigley, curatorial assistant, for help with every aspect of the exhibition's preparation. The Institute's Advisory Board, who supported the entire endeavor from the very first, has been a constant source of encouragement. Although the original installation plan was mine—in part governed by ICA's space, artists' requirements, and standardized building materials—its ultimate form came from roundtable discussions with Michael A. Quigley, John Taylor and Gregory Tobias. Thankfully we received many suggestions about acoustics from Sidney Dorfman at Ace Lumber and Millworks in Philadelphia. The installation structures were skillfully built by Randall

Dalton, Thomas Nicholas, John Taylor and Gregory Tobias; they were assisted by Bill Bauman, James Juszczyk, Pierre Payne and Joseph Ross. Many of our technical problems were solved during the initial planning stages thanks to advice from Peter Voetsch as well as from Tom Harding and Michael Kowalski at Smith, Kline and French. The closed-circuit system for presenting videotapes was masterfully supervised by Curt Carlson from VideoPlay Industries in Rockville, Connecticut. We are appreciative of Tim Tasker from the School of Architecture, who volunteered to help with countless last minute details.

Raymond Kullman and John Davis from the University's Department of Buildings and Grounds good-naturedly attended to our complicated electrical needs. Les Levine's *Contact* was ably installed by Peter Cuozzo, Starrship Associates, Inc., Philadelphia. Our deep appreciation goes to Allan F. Hofmann, coordinator of visual communications at the University's School of Dental Medicine, for overseeing the maintenance of VIDEO ART's technical system; his ready aid kept everything running with blessed smoothness. Carla Hultman, Charles Rosenberg and Cranston Walker—ICA gallery attendants—cheerfully assumed the added burden of daily equipment care.

This publication, which hopefully will serve as a useful document of the artists' exploration of video, is the result of the contributions and devotion of many persons. I would like to extend my deepest appreciation to David Antin, Lizzie Borden, Jack Burnham and John McHale for their essays. The bibliography was assembled by Michael A. Quigley; Nancy Blum did much of the initial legwork for the bibliography. My affectionate thanks to Christine LaValley, Marcia Olives, Gayle Samuels and Debra Steffani for typing the catalogue copy and for handling the masses of correspondence the project required. We are most grateful to Sarah Williams, who served as the publication's editorial advisor, for her unerring sense of clarity, and to Lynn Lewis for her eagle eye. I also wish to extend my particular thanks to Eugene Feldman and Falcon Press for printing this publication; his skill, calm logic and special interest in video made the entire production a pleasure. The exhibition poster was designed by Bill Sontag of The Contemporary Arts Center in Cincinnati.

A project as complicated and costly as VIDEO ART would not have been possible for ICA and the three participating institutions without a generous grant from the National Endowment for the Arts in Washington, D.C.. We gratefully acknowledge the Endowment's support as well as grants from the Commonwealth of Pennsylvania Council on the Arts and The Philadelphia Foundation, which provided a substantial share of the Institute's matching funds. Such support has allowed the Institute the particular privilege of organizing VIDEO ART for audiences in metropolitan Philadelphia. We are also honored to present this exhibition to wider audiences through the collaboration of The Contemporary Arts Center, the Museum of Contemporary Art and the Wadsworth Atheneum.

Suzanne Delehanty
Director
Institute of Contemporary Art
University of Pennsylvania

THE ARTISTS

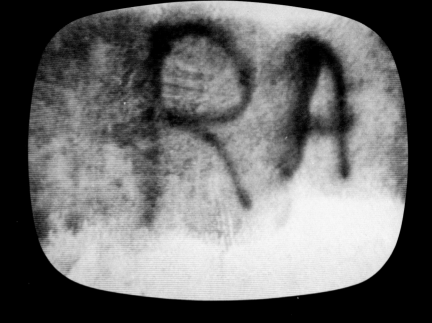

Vito Acconci Born 1940 in the Bronx, New York. Lives in New York. **Selected Individual Exhibitions** 1969 Carr House Gallery, Rhode Island School of Design, Providence, Rhode Island. 1970 Wesleyan University, Middletown, Connecticut; Nova Scotia College of Art and Design, Halifax, Nova Scotia. 1971 Museum of Conceptual Art, San Francisco. 1972 California Institute of the Arts, Valencia, California. **Selected Exhibitions and Events** 1969 *Language III* Dwan Gallery, New York; *Street Works I-IV* Architectural League of New York, New York; *Aleph 70* New York University, New York; *587,087* The Seattle Art Museum, Seattle, Washington. 1970 *955,000* Vancouver Art Gallery, Vancouver, British Columbia; *Art in the Mind* Allen Memorial Art Museum, Oberlin College, Oberlin, Ohio; *Information* The Museum of Modern Art, New York; *Software* The Jewish Museum, New York; *Recorded Activities* Moore College of Art, Philadelphia. 1971 *Body Art* John Gibson Gallery, New York; *Projected Art* Finch College Museum of Art, New York; *Sonsbeek '71* Arnhem, The Netherlands; *Systems Art* Museo de Arte Moderno, Buenos Aires; *Pier 18* The Museum of Modern Art, New York; *Prospect '71: Projection* Kunsthalle, Düsseldorf; *Artists' Videotape Performances* Finch College Museum of Art, New York. 1972 *Notes and Scores for Sound* Mills College Art Museum, Oakland, California; *Documenta 5* Kassel, West Germany. 1973 *Contemporanea* Rome. 1974 *Art Now '74* John F. Kennedy Center for the Performing ARTS, Washington, D.C.; *Project '74* Cologne.

Sonia Andrade Born 1935 in Rio de Janeiro. 1973-74 Studied with Anna Bella Geiger at the Museum of Modern Art, Rio de Janeiro. Lives in Rio de Janeiro. **Selected Exhibitions** 1974 *Summer Salon* Museu de Belas Artes, Rio de Janeiro; *Prospective '74* Museu de Arte Contemporânea da Universidade de São Paulo, São Paulo; *Young Contemporary Art* Museu de Arte Contemporânea da Universidade de São Paulo, São Paulo.

Ant Farm

Chip Lord Born 1944 in Cleveland, Ohio. B. Arch. 1948 Tulane University, New Orleans, Louisiana. Lives in San Francisco. **Hudson Marquez** Born 1946 in New Orleans, Louisiana. Attended Newcomb School of Art, Tulane University, New Orleans. Lives in San Francisco. **Doug Michels** Born 1943 in Seattle, Washington. B. Arch. 1967 School of Architecture, Yale University, New Haven, Connecticut. 1973 Design Award citation from *Progressive Architecture*. Lives in San Francisco. **Curtis Schreier** Born 1944 in Philadelphia. Graduated 1967 Rhode Island School of Design, Providence, Rhode Island. **Group History** Ant Farm was founded in 1968 by Chip Lord and Doug Michels to work in architecture and allied arts. In 1970 they were joined by Hudson Marquez and Curtis Schreier. Ant Farm began using videotape in 1971 as an adjunct to architectural projects. As graphic artists, the group has contributed to *Radical Software*. **Selected Exhibitions** 1969 *Biennale* Paris. 1973 *20-20 Vision* Contemporary Arts Museum, Houston, Texas. **Broadcast** *The Cadillac Ranch Show* WPII-TV Amarillo, Texas.

Eleanor Antin Born 1935 in New York. BA City College of New York. Graduate study in philosophy, New School for Social Research, New York. Studied theater at Tamara Daykarhanova School for the Stage, New York. Lives in Solana Beach, California.   **Selected Individual Exhibitions** 1972 *Library Science* Nova Scotia College of Art and Design, Halifax, Nova Scotia. 1973 *Part of an Autobiography* Portland Center for the Visual Arts, Portland, Oregon; *100 Boots* The Museum of Modern Art, New York. 1974 *The Ballerina and the King* Galleriaforma, Genoa, Italy; *Narratives* Centro de Arte y Comunicación, Buenos Aires; *Several Selves* Everson Museum of Art, Syracuse, New York. 1975 Stefanotty Gallery, New York.   **Selected Group Exhibitions** 1969 *Language III* Dwan Gallery, New York. 1971 *Systems Art* Museo de Arte Moderno, Buenos Aires; *Image Bank Post Card Show* Art Gallery, University of British Columbia, Vancouver, British Columbia; *Biennale* Paris. 1972 *Encuentros* Pamplona, Spain; *Invisible/Visible* Long Beach Museum of Art, Long Beach, California; *Bienal de Arte Coltejer* Medellin, Colombia. 1973 *Opening Invitational* Womanspace, Los Angeles; *Dimensional Prints* Los Angeles County Museum of Art, Los Angeles; *Art of the '70s* Xerox Square Center, Rochester, New York; *Projection* Ursula Wevers, Cologne. 1974 *Flash Art* Kunstverein, Cologne; *Focus—American Art 1974* Museum of the Philadelphia Civic Center, Philadelphia; *Project '74* Cologne; *Autobiography* ArtSpace, New York. **Events** 1972 *Avant-Garde Festival* New York. 1974 *Black Is Beautiful* University of California, Irvine; *Eleanor-1954* Womanspace, Los Angeles.

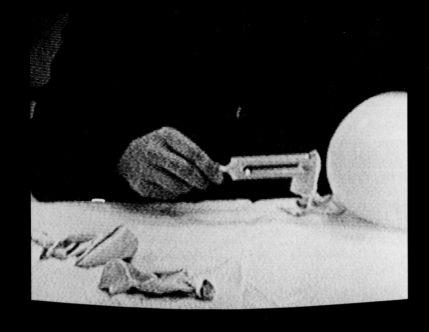

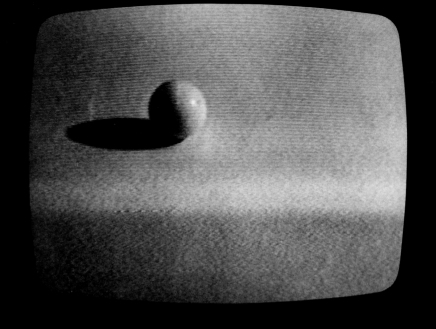

David Askevold Born 1940 in Conrad, Montana. Studied at University of Montana, Missoula, Montana; Brooklyn Museum School of Art, Brooklyn; Kansas City Art Institute, Kansas City. Lives in Halifax, Nova Scotia **Selected Individual Exhibitions** 1970 Nova Scotia College of Art and Design, Halifax, Nova Scotia. 1972 *Art and Project,* Amsterdam; Galerie Paul Maenz, Cologne; Jack Wendler, London. **Selected Group Exhibitions** 1970 *Information* The Museum of Modern Art, New York; *3,549,000* Centro de Arte y Comunicación, Buenos Aires. 1971 A Space, Toronto; Cheltenham Township Art Center, Cheltenham, Pennsylvania; *Pier 18* The Museum of Modern Art, New York. 1972 Museum of Conceptual Art, San Francisco. 1973 *Story* John Gibson Gallery, New York. 1974 *Narrative II* John Gibson Gallery, New York; *Project '74* Cologne; *Videoscape* Art Gallery of Ontario, Toronto.

John Baldessari Born 1931 in National City, California. BA 1953 San Diego State College, San Diego, California. MA 1957 San Diego State College, San Diego, California. Lives in Santa Monica, California. **Selected Individual Exhibitions** 1964 La Jolla Museum of Art, La Jolla, California. 1968 Molly Barnes Gallery, Los Angeles. 1970 Richard Feigen Gallery, New York. 1971 Galerie Konrad Fischer, Düsseldorf; Nova Scotia College of Art and Design, Halifax, Nova Scotia. 1972 Gallery Toselli, Milan. 1973 Sonnabend Gallery, New York. 1974 Galerie MTL, Brussels. **Selected Group Exhibitions** 1969 *Art by Telephone* Museum of Contemporary Art, Chicago; *Annual* Whitney Museum of American Art, New York; *Language III* Dwan Gallery, New York; *Konzeption-Conception* Städtisches Museum, Leverkusen, West Germany. 1970 *Recorded Activities* Moore College of Art, Philadelphia; *Art in the Mind* Allen Memorial Art Gallery, Oberlin College, Oberlin, Ohio; *Software* The Jewish Museum, New York; *Information* The Museum of Modern Art, New York. 1971 *Prospect '71: Projection* Kunsthalle, Düsseldorf; *Pier 18* The Museum of Modern Art, New York. 1972 *Documenta 5* Kassel, West Germany; *Koncept-Kunst* Kunstmuseum, Basel, Switzerland; *Biennale* Venice; *St. Jude Video Invitational* de Saisset Art Gallery and Museum, University of Santa Clara, Santa Clara, California; *Southern California Attitudes* Pasadena Museum of Art, Pasadena, California; *Biennial* Whitney Museum of American Art, New York. 1973 *Circuit: A Video Invitational* Everson Museum of Art, Syracuse, New York. 1974 *Project '74* Cologne.

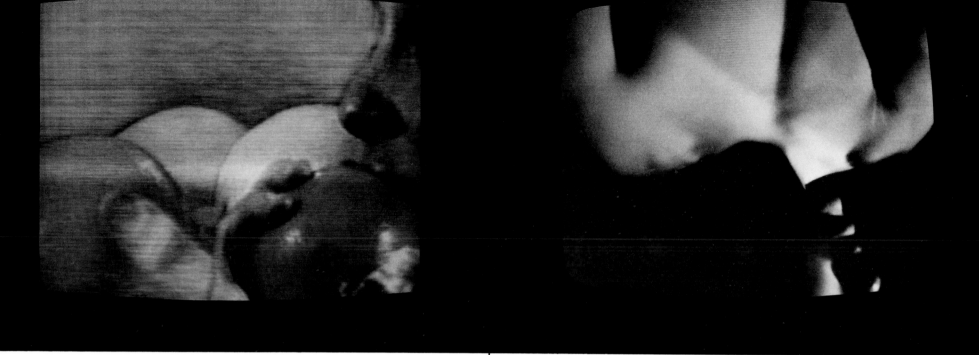

Lynda Benglis Born 1941 in Lake Charles, Louisiana. BFA 1964 Newcomb College, New Orleans, Louisiana. Lives in New York. **Selected Individual Exhibitions** 1969 University of Rhode Island, Kingston, Rhode Island. 1970 Paula Cooper Gallery, New York; Janie C. Lee Gallery, Dallas, Texas. 1971 Hayden Gallery, Massachusetts Institute of Technology, Cambridge, Massachusetts. 1972 Hansen-Fuller Gallery, San Francisco. 1973 Everson Museum of Art, Syracuse, New York. 1974 The Clocktower, New York. **Selected Group Exhibitions** 1969 *Other Ideas* The Detroit Institute of Art, Detroit; *Prospect '69* Düsseldorf; *Art and Process IV* Finch College Museum of Art, New York. 1971 *Twenty-Six by Twenty-Six* Vassar College, Poughkeepsie, New York; *Works for New Spaces* Walker Art Center, Minneapolis, Minnesota. 1972 *American Women Artists Show* GEDOK, Kunsthaus, Hamburg; *Painting: New Options* Walker Art Center, Minneapolis, Minnesota; *Painting & Sculpture Today* Indianapolis Museum of Art, Indianapolis, Indiana; *32nd Annual Exhibition* The Art Institute of Chicago, Chicago; *St. Jude Video Invitational* de Saisset Art Gallery and Museum, University of Santa Clara, Santa Clara, California. 1973 *Biennial* Whitney Museum of American Art, New York; *Circuit: A Video Invitational* Everson Museum of Art, Syracuse, New York; *Options and Alternatives* Yale University Art Gallery, New Haven, Connecticut; *Option 73/30: Recent Works of Art* Contemporary Arts Center, Cincinnati, Ohio. 1974 *Project '74* Cologne; *Project: Video* The Museum of Modern Art, New York.

Jim Byrne Born 1950 in Chisago City, Minnesota. Studied University of Minnesota, Minneapolis, Minnesota. Lives in Minneapolis. **Selected Individual Exhibitions** 1975 The Kitchen, New York. **Selected Group Exhibitions** 1974 *New Learning Spaces and Places* Walker Art Center, Minneapolis, Minnesota. 1975 *Akagawa/Byrne* Walker Art Center, Minneapolis, Minnesota; *Biennial* Whitney Museum of American Art, New York.

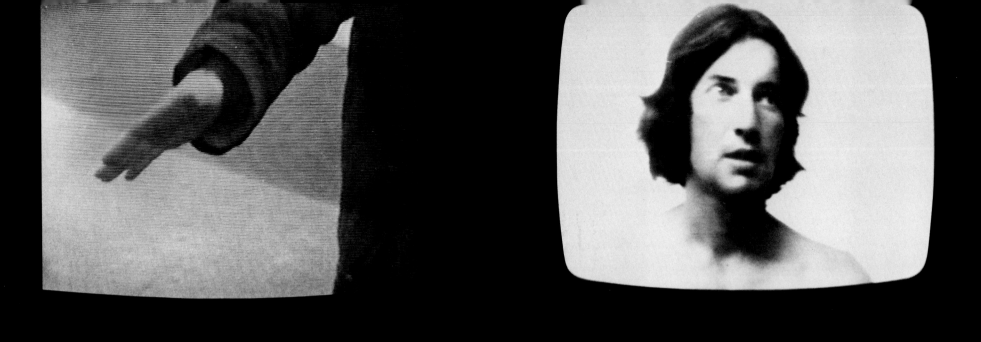

Pierpaolo Calzolari   Born 1943 in Bologna, Italy. Lives in Berlin.
Individual Exhibitions 1965 Sala Studio Bentivoglio, Bologna. 1967
Sala Studio Bentivoglio, Bologna. 1969 Galleria Sperone, Turin. 1970
Galerie Ileana Sonnabend, Paris. 1971 Modern Art Agency, Naples.
Selected Group Exhibitions 1966 Ca' Giustinina, Venice. 1968
Lavori nell'aria e nella terra Varese; *Teatro delle Mostre* Galleria La
Tartaruga, Rome; *Arte Povera* Galleria De'Foscherari, Bologna. 1969
Square Pegs in Round Holes Stedelijk Museum, Amsterdam; *When
Attitude Becomes Form* Kunsthalle, Bern; *Konzeption/Conception*
Städtisches Museum, Leverkusen, West Germany. 1970 *Conceptual
Art/Arte Povera/Land Art* Galleria Civica d'Arte Moderna, Turin; *Processi di pensiero visualizzati* Kunst Museum, Lucerne; *Biennale Internazionale della Giovane Pittura* Museo Civico, Bologna. 1971
Biennale Paris; *Informazioni sulla presenza italiana* Incontri Internazionali d'Arte, Rome. 1972 *Documenta 5* Kassel, West Germany.
1974 *Project '74* Cologne. 1975 *Americans in Florence: Europeans in
Florence* Long Beach Museum of Art, Long Beach, California.

Colin Campbell   Born 1942 Reston, Manitoba. BFA 1966 University of Manitoba, Winnipeg. MFA 1969 Claremont Graduate School,
Claremont, California. Lives in Sackville, New Brunswick. **Selected
Individual Exhibitions** 1969 Pomona College, Claremont, California. 1972 Nova Scotia College of Art and Design, Halifax, Nova
Scotia. 1973 A Space, Toronto. 1974 A Space, Toronto; Memorial Art
Gallery, University of Rochester, Rochester, New York. **Selected
Group Exhibitions** 1971 Owens Art Gallery, Sackville, New
Brunswick. 1973 *Video Circuits* University of Guelph, Guelph, Ontario. 1974 *Toronto Video Artists* Everson Museum of Art, Syracuse,
New York; *Project '74* Cologne; *Videoscape* Art Gallery of Ontario,
Toronto. 1975 *Biennale* Paris.

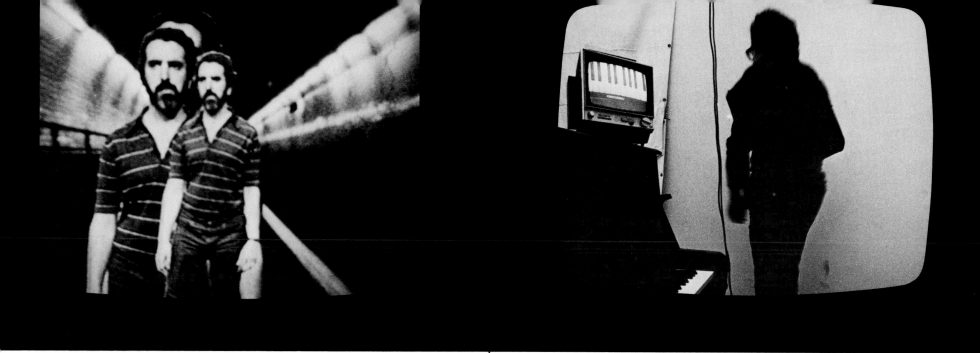

Peter Campus   Born 1937 in New York. B.S. in Psychology Ohio State University, Columbus, Ohio. Attended Film Institute, City College of New York, New York. Lives in New York.   **Selected Individual Exhibitions**   1972 Bykert Gallery, New York.   1973 Bykert Gallery, New York.   1974 Everson Museum of Art, Syracuse, New York; The Kitchen, New York.   **Selected Group Exhibitions**   1972 *Projected Art* Finch College Museum of Art, New York and The Corcoran Gallery of Art, Washington, D.C.; Bykert Gallery, New York.   1973 *Biennial* Whitney Museum of American Art, New York; *Circuit: A Video Invitational* Everson Museum of Art, Syracuse, New York; *Bienal* São Paulo; *Re-Vision* Contemporary Arts Museum, Houston, Texas.   1974 Leo Castelli Gallery, New York; The Kitchen, New York; *Project '74* Cologne; Artpark, Lewiston, New York; *New Learning Spaces and Places* Walker Art Center, Minneapolis, Minnesota; *Projected Images* Walker Art Center, Minneapolis, Minnesota; *Art Now '74* John F. Kennedy Center for the Performing Arts, Washington, D.C.   **Broadcasts**   1973 *Three Transitions* WGBH-TV Boston.   1974 *R-G-B* The Television Laboratory, WNET-TV New York; *Set of Coincidence* WGBH-TV Boston.

Giuseppe Chiari   Born 1926 in Florence. Studied mathematics and music. Lives in Florence.   **Selected Performances**   1962 Galleria Numero, Rome; Galleria La Salita, Rome; *Fluxus Festival* Wiesbaden.   1963 *Avant-Garde Festival* New York; Galleria Blu, Milan; *Fluxus Festival* Paris.   1964 *Avant-Garde Festival* New York; *Fluxus Festival* New York.   1965 Galerie Parnass, Wuppertal, West Germany; Institute of Contemporary Arts, London.   1966 Galerie René Block, Berlin; *Festival de la Libre Expression* Paris.   1967 *Avant-Garde Festival* New York.   1968 Film Akademie, Berlin; *Pro Musica Nuova* Radio Bremen, West Germany.   1970 Teatro La Fede, Rome; Film-Studio, Rome.   1971 Modern Art Agency, Naples.   1972 *Documenta 5* Kassel, West Germany.   1975 *Americans in Florence: Europeans in Florence* Long Beach Museum of Art, Long Beach, California.

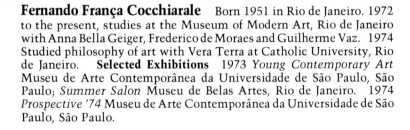

Fernando França Cocchiarale   Born 1951 in Rio de Janeiro. 1972
to the present, studies at the Museum of Modern Art, Rio de Janeiro
with Anna Bella Geiger, Frederico de Moraes and Guilherme Vaz. 1974
Studied philosophy of art with Vera Terra at Catholic University, Rio
de Janeiro.   **Selected Exhibitions**   1973 *Young Contemporary Art*
Museu de Arte Contemporânea da Universidade de São Paulo, São
Paulo; *Summer Salon* Museu de Belas Artes, Rio de Janeiro. 1974
Prospective '74 Museu de Arte Contemporânea da Universidade de São
Paulo, São Paulo.

Andrea Daninos   Born in Italy. Lives in Florence.   **Selected Exhibitions** 1974 *Project '74* Cologne.

This is a real-time
                    videotape.
The performance you are
                    watching
has occured
            is occuring
in real time your time
                    no editing.

Douglas Davis Born 1938 in Washington, D.C. BA 1956 American University, Washington, D.C. MA 1958 Rutgers—The State University, New Brunswick, New Jersey. Lives in New York. **Selected Individual Exhibitions** 1972 Everson Museum of Art, Syracuse, New York; The Kitchen, New York. 1973 Finch College Museum of Art, New York; St. Jude Video Invitational de Saisset Art Gallery and Museum, University of Santa Clara, Santa Clara, California. 1974 Fischbach Gallery, New York. **Selected Group Exhibitions** 1970 *Projected Art* Finch College Museum of Art, New York. 1971 *Ten Videotape Performances* Finch College Museum of Art, New York; *Video Free America* University Art Museum, University of California, Berkeley. 1974 *St. Jude Video Invitational* de Saisset Art Gallery and Museum, University of Santa Clara, Santa Clara, California. *Art/Video Confrontation 74* Musée d'Art Moderne de la Ville de Paris, Paris; *Art As Living Ritual* Neue Galerie am Joanneum Landesmuseum, Graz, Austria; *Video/Art/Impact* Galerie Impact, Lausanne, Switzerland; *Editions Video Distribution* Galerie Germain, Paris; *Project '74* Cologne; *Art Now '74* John F. Kennedy Center for the Performing Arts, Washington, D.C. **Selected Broadcasts** 1970 *"Numbers: A Videotape Event"* WGBH-TV Boston for *Video Variations.* 1971 *Electronic Hokkadim,* a two-way telecast, WTOP-TV and The Corcoran Gallery of Art, Washington, D.C. 1972 *Talk-Out!* WGNY-TV and Everson Museum of Art, Syracuse, New York. 1974 *The Austrian Tapes* ORF-TV Austria.

Antonio Dias Born 1944 in Paraíba, Brazil. 1971 Guggenheim Fellowship. Lives in Milan. **Selected Individual Exhibitions** 1962 Galeria Sorbradinho, Rio de Janeiro. 1964 Galeria Relêvo, Rio de Janeiro. 1965 Galerie Houston-Brown, Paris. 1966 Galeria Guignard, Belo Horizonte. 1967 Galerie Delta, Rotterdam. 1969 Studio Marconi, Milan. 1971 Galleria Breton, Milan. 1972 Galeria Stampa, Basel, Switzerland. 1973 Galeria Ralph Camargo, São Paulo; Bôlsa de Arte, Rio de Janeiro; Centro de Arte y Comunicación, Buenos Aires. 1974 Galerie Nächst St. Stephan, Vienna. **Selected Group Exhibitions** 1965 *Salon de la Jeune Peinture* Musée d'Art Moderne de la Ville de Paris, Paris; *Jovem Pintura* Museu de Arte Contemporânea da Universidade de São Paulo, São Paulo; *Opinion 65* Museu de Arte Moderna, Rio de Janeiro; *Biennale* Paris. 1966 *Brazilian Vanguard* Universidade de Minas Gerais, Belo Horizonte; *Contemporary Brazilian Art* Museo Arte Moderno, Buenos Aires. 1967 *The World in Question* Musée d'Art Moderne de la Ville de Paris, Paris; *Science Fiction* Kunsthalle, Bern, Switzerland. 1969 *Art-Dialogue Between the East and the West* National Museum of Art, Tokyo; *Plan and Project in Art* Kunsthalle, Bern, Switzerland. 1970 *Activities, Projects, Thoughts* Museo Civico, Bologna; *Art and Politics* Kunstverein, Karlsruhe, West Germany. 1971 *6th International Exhibition* The Solomon R. Guggenheim Museum, New York. 1972 *Systems Art II* Museo de Arte Moderno, Buenos Aires. 1973 *Expo-Projection-Audio-Visual* GRIFA, São Paulo. 1974 *Flash Art* Kunstverein, Cologne; *Project '74* Cologne.

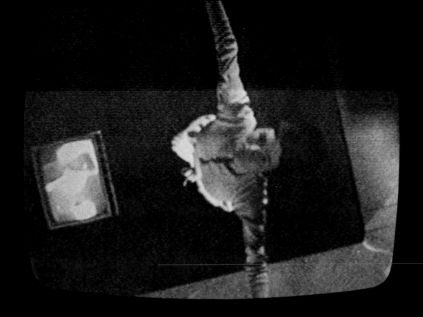
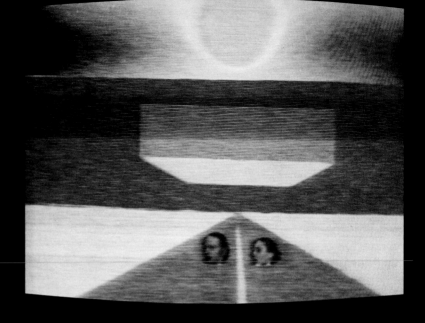

Juan Downey Born 1940 in Santiago, Chile. B.Arch. 1961 School of Architecture, Catholic University of Chile, Santiago. Studied 1963-65 with Stanley Hayter, Atelier 17, Paris. Lives in New York. **Selected Individual Exhibitions** 1965 Pan American Union, Washington, D.C.; Casa de las Americas, Havana. 1968 Judson Gallery, New York. 1969 The Corcoran Gallery of Art, Washington, D.C. 1970 *With Energy Beyond These Walls* Howard Wise Gallery, New York. 1971 *Life Cycle* The Electric Gallery, Toronto. 1973 Everson Museum of Art, Syracuse, New York. 1974 *Publicness* The Kitchen, New York. **Selected Group Exhibitions** 1964 *Salon de Mai* Musée d'Art Moderne de la Ville de Paris, Paris. 1965 *Artisti Latinoamericani d'Avanguardia* Galleria Due Mondi, Rome. 1966 *The Hard-Edge Trend* National Collection of Fine Arts, Smithsonian Institution, Washington, D.C. 1968 *Some More Beginnings E.A.T.* The Brooklyn Museum, Brooklyn, New York. 1969 *Cybernetic Serendipity* Institute of Contemporary Arts, London. 1970 *Air* Victoria Museum, Melbourne, Australia. 1971 *Art and Science* Tel Aviv Museum, Tel Aviv. 1972 *Making Megalopolis Understandable* The New York Cultural Center, New York. 1973 *Circuit: A Video Invitational* Everson Museum of Art, Syracuse, New York. 1974 *Art Now '74* John F. Kennedy Center for the Performing Arts, Washington, D.C.; *Project '74* Cologne. **Broadcast** 1974 *Chilean Flag* Channel D, Manhattan Cable TV, New York.

Ed Emshwiller Born 1939 in New York. BA 1949 University of Michigan, Ann Arbor, Michigan. Attended 1949-50 École des Beaux-Arts, Paris and Art Students League, New York. Filmmaker in Residence 1970 Cornell University, Ithaca, New York. Artist in Residence 1973 WNET-TV New York; Guggenheim Fellowship. Lives in Wantaugh, New York. **Selected Group Exhibitions** 1971 *Video Show* Whitney Museum of American Art, New York. 1972 *1st National Videotape Festival* Minnesota College of Art and Design, Minneapolis, Minnesota; *Computer Image Festival* The Kitchen, New York. 1973 The Kitchen, New York; *Circuit: A Video Invitational* Everson Museum of Art, Syracuse, New York; American Cultural Center, Tokyo; American Cultural Center, Paris. 1974 *Open Circuits: The Future of Television* The Museum of Modern Art, New York. **Selected Film Showings** 1967 *Oberhausen Festival* Oberhausen, West Germany. 1969 *Cine-Probe* The Museum of Modern Art, New York. 1970 *Brussels Festival* Brussels; *Mannheim Festival* Mannheim, West Germany. 1972 *Cine-Probe* The Museum of Modern Art, New York. 1973 *Berlin Film Festival* Berlin. **Selected Broadcasts** 1973 *Scape-Mates* WNET-TV New York. 1974 *Philobolus and Joan* WNET-TV New York.

Valie Export Born 1942 in Linz, Austria. Studied art in Linz and design in Vienna. Founding member of Austria Filmmakers' Cooperative. Member of Institute for Direct Art, Vienna. Lives in Vienna. **Selected Film Showings** 1969 *Multi-Media I* Vienna; *Underground Explosion* Munich; *Krone Circus* Zurich; Volkshaus, Cologne. 1970 *First International Underground Film Festival* London; *Viennale '70* Vienna. 1971 *Experimenta 4* Frankfurt. 1972 Cinematheque, Liège, Belgium. 1973 *Festival of Independent Avant-Garde Film* National Film Theatre, London. **Selected Group Exhibitions** 1973 *Austrian Exhibition* Edinburgh Festival, Edinburgh; *Trigon '73* Neue Galerie am Landesmuseum Joanneum, Graz, Austria; *Body Language* Neue Galerie am Landesmuseum Joanneum, Graz, Austria. 1974 *Flash Art* Kunstverein, Cologne; *Project '74* Cologne; *Video/Art/Impact* Galerie Impact, Lausanne, Switzerland.

Terry Fox Born 1943 in Seattle, Washington. Attended 1961 Cornish School of Allied Arts, Seattle, Washington. Attended 1962-63 Accademia di Belli Arti, Rome. Lives in San Francisco. **Selected Individual Exhibitions** 1970 Reese Palley Gallery, San Francisco; Museum of Conceptual Art, San Francisco. 1972 Modern Art Agency, Naples. 1973 University Art Museum, University of California, Berkeley. 1974 Everson Museum of Art, Syracuse, New York. 1975 *Art/Tapes/22* Florence. **Selected Group Exhibitions** 1970 *The Eighties* University Art Museum, University of California, Berkeley. 1971 *Pier 18* The Museum of Modern Art, New York; *Systems Art* Museo de Arte Moderno, Buenos Aires; *Prospect '71: Projection* Kunsthalle, Düsseldorf. 1972 *Notes and Scores for Sound* Mills College Art Museum, Oakland, California; *San Francisco Performance* Newport Harbor Art Museum, Newport Beach, California; *Bienal de Arte Coltejer* Medellin, Colombia; *Encuentros* Pamplona, Spain; *Video West* Everson Museum of Art, Syracuse, New York; *Systems Art II* Museo de Arte Moderno, Buenos Aires; *St. Jude Video Invitational* de Saisset Art Gallery and Museum, University of Santa Clara, Santa Clara, California; *Documenta 5* Kassel, West Germany. 1973 *Video* Kunststichting, Rotterdam; *Circuit: A Video Invitational* Everson Museum of Art, Syracuse, New York. 1974 *Collectors' Video* Los Angeles County Museum of Art, Los Angeles; *Art Now '74* John F. Kennedy Center for the Performing Arts, Washington, D.C.; *Flash Art* Kunstverein, Cologne; *Project '74* Cologne.

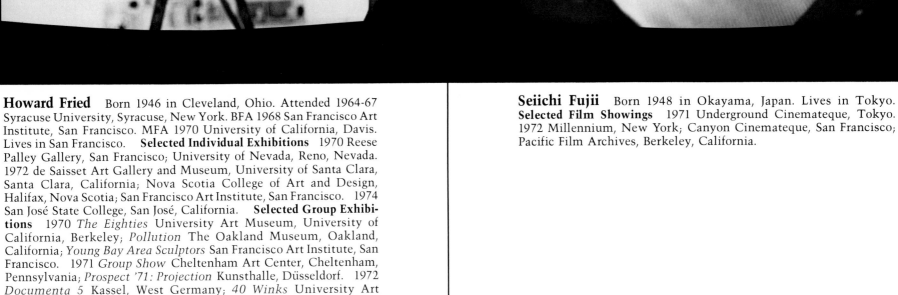

Howard Fried Born 1946 in Cleveland, Ohio. Attended 1964-67 Syracuse University, Syracuse, New York. BFA 1968 San Francisco Art Institute, San Francisco. MFA 1970 University of California, Davis. Lives in San Francisco. **Selected Individual Exhibitions** 1970 Reese Palley Gallery, San Francisco; University of Nevada, Reno, Nevada. 1972 de Saisset Art Gallery and Museum, University of Santa Clara, Santa Clara, California; Nova Scotia College of Art and Design, Halifax, Nova Scotia; San Francisco Art Institute, San Francisco. 1974 San José State College, San José, California. **Selected Group Exhibitions** 1970 *The Eighties* University Art Museum, University of California, Berkeley; *Pollution* The Oakland Museum, Oakland, California; *Young Bay Area Sculptors* San Francisco Art Institute, San Francisco. 1971 *Group Show* Cheltenham Art Center, Cheltenham, Pennsylvania; *Prospect '71: Projection* Kunsthalle, Düsseldorf. 1972 *Documenta 5* Kassel, West Germany; *40 Winks* University Art Museum, University of California, Berkeley; *Notes and Scores for Sound* Mills College Art Museum, Oakland, California; *St. Jude Video Invitational* de Saisset Art Gallery and Museum, University of Santa Clara, Santa Clara, California; *San Francisco Performance* Newport Harbor Art Museum, Newport Beach, California; *Video West* Everson Museum of Art, Syracuse, New York. 1974 *Project '74* Cologne; *Steven A. Davis, Howard Fried, Steven Kaltenbach* University Art Museum, University of California, Berkeley. **Broadcast** 1974 *Actions by Sculptors for the Home Audience* KQED-TV San Francisco.

Seiichi Fujii Born 1948 in Okayama, Japan. Lives in Tokyo. **Selected Film Showings** 1971 Underground Cinemateque, Tokyo. 1972 Millennium, New York; Canyon Cinemateque, San Francisco; Pacific Film Archives, Berkeley, California.

Anna Bella Geiger   Born 1933 in Rio de Janeiro. Studied 1951-53 drawing and art history with Fayga Ostrower. Studied 1953-57 Anglo-Saxon languages at National Faculty of Philosophy, Rio de Janeiro. 1954-55 Lived in Toronto. 1970-72 Published "Dialectics and Metavanguard," "Unconscious and Consumption," "A Concept for the SNAV" (Institute for Visual Arts) in *O Jornal do Brasil*. 1970-73 Member, Cultural Commission, Museum of Modern Art, Rio de Janeiro. 1973 Organized classes entitled *A Journey from the Object to the Body* and *The House, the City—a Support to Images, Myths and Symbols*. Lives in Rio de Janeiro.   **Selected Group Exhibitions** 1967 *Biennial of Young Painters* Musée d'Art Moderne de la Ville de Paris, Paris; *Bienal* São Paulo.   1973 *Expo-Projection-Audio Visual* GRIFE, São Paulo.   1974 *Prospective '74* Museu de Arte Contemporânea da Universidade de São Paulo, São Paulo.

Michael Geissler and Video Audio Medien

Michael Geissler   Born 1942 in Berlin. After working as a traveling sales representative, attended the Academy for Graphic Arts and Film Processing, Berlin, and the German Film and Television Academy, Berlin. Lives in Berlin. **Dörte Võtz**   Born in Frankfurt/Oder. 1961 fled to West Berlin and studied medicine. Worked as film cutter for Schamoni and Lemke among others. 1970-71 studied German Film and Television Academy, Berlin. **Lena Conradt**   Born 1942 in Stuttgart. 1962-67 studied acting and worked in the theater. 1968-70 translated film scripts and worked on films produced at German Film and Television Academy, Berlin. Lives in Berlin. In addition to Geissler, Võtz and Conradt, VAM has a rotating company including Peno Blankschein, J. Paul Getty III, Lothar Lambert, Mackay Taylor, Jutta Zacher, Martina Zacher and others.   **Group History**   Since 1971 VAM has created non-fiction television programs on hospitals, education, immigrant workers, group therapy, and resocialized drug addicts. **Selected Broadcasts**   1971 *Behind the Scenes of a Second Class Caberet*.   1972 *We Have to Be the White Indians of Europe*.   1973 *Children and Art; Interview with John Vaccaro/Berlin's Reaction to the New Theater of the Absurd*.   1974 *Berlin by the Wall; German Rock*.

General Idea

Ron Gabe   Born 1945. BFA 1967 University of Manitoba, School of Art, Winnipeg, Manitoba. Artist in Residence 1972 University of Saskatchewan, Regina, Saskatchewan. Lives in Toronto. **Jorge Saia**   Born 1944. B. Arch. 1968 Dalhousie University, Halifax, Nova Scotia. Lives in Toronto. **Michael Tims**   Born 1946. Lecturer 1968 University of Manitoba, Winnipeg, Manitoba. Director 1969 Théâtre Passé Muraille, Toronto. Art director 1970 Festival of Underground Theatre, St. Lawrence Centre for the Arts, Toronto. Lives in Toronto. **Group History**   In 1968 Ron Gabe, Jorge Saia, and Michael Tims formed General Idea to work together in a variety of media. In 1971 General Idea established Art Official, Inc. and began publishing *File Magazine*. In 1974 they opened Art Metropole, a library and distribution center for artists' publications and videotapes.   **Selected Exhibitions**   1970 *Concept '70* Nightingale Gallery, Toronto; *The 1970 Miss General Idea Pageant* St. Lawrence Centre for the Arts, Toronto.   1971 *Image Bank Postcard Show* Art Gallery of Ontario, Toronto.   1972 *Light On* Carman Lamanna Gallery, Toronto; *Expose* A Space Gallery, Toronto; *Evidence of Body Binding* Gallery B, Montreal.   1973 *Realism: Emulsion and Emission* Agnes Etherington Art Gallery, Kingston, Ontario; *Canada Trajectoires* Musée d'Art Moderne de la Ville de Paris, Paris.   1974 *Project '74* Cologne; *Art's Birthday* Hollywood, California; *General Idea at Western Front* Vancouver, British Columbia; *Videoscape* Art Gallery of Ontario, Toronto.

Frank Gillette   Born 1941 in Jersey City, New Jersey. Studied painting 1952-62 Pratt Institute, New York.   1973 Published *Between Paradigms*. Lives in New York.   **Selected Individual Exhibitions** 1973 Everson Museum of Art, Syracuse, New York.   1974 *Art/Tapes/22* Florence; The Kitchen, New York.   **Selected Group Exhibitions** 1969 *TV As a Creative Medium* Howard Wise Gallery, New York. 1970 *Vision and Television* Rose Art Museum, Brandeis University, Waltham, Massachusetts.   1971 *Air* Everson Museum of Art, Syracuse, New York.   1972 *St. Jude Video International* de Saisset Art Gallery and Museum, University of Santa Clara, Santa Clara, California.   1973 *Circuit: A Video Invitational* Everson Museum of Art, Syracuse, New York; *Bienal* São Paulo.   1974 *New Learning Spaces and Places* Walker Art Center, Minneapolis, Minnesota; *Collectors' Video* Los Angeles County Museum of Art, Los Angeles; Leo Castelli Gallery, New York; *Art Now '74* John F. Kennedy Center for the Performing Arts, Washington, D.C.; *Project '74* Cologne; *Art/Video Confrontation 74* Musée d'Art Moderne de la Ville de Paris, Paris; *Video As an Art Form* Smith College Museum of Art, Northampton, Massachusetts; *Americans in Florence: Europeans in Florence* Long Beach Museum of Art, Long Beach, California.

Dan Graham   Born 1942 in Urbana, Illinois. Lives in New York.
Selected Individual Exhibitions   1970 Nova Scotia College of Art and
Design, Halifax, Nova Scotia.   1972 Lisson Gallery, London; Toselli
Gallery, Milan.   1973 Galerie MTL, Brussels; Galleria Schema, Flor-
ence.   1974 Galerie MTL, Brussels; Galerie 17, Paris; Galerie 20, Paris;
The Royal College of Art, London.   **Selected Group Exhibitions**   1966
Projected Art Finch College Museum of Art, New York; *Working
drawings and other visible things on paper not necessarily meant to be
viewed as art* The School of Visual Arts, New York.   1967 *Art in a
Series* Finch College Museum of Art, New York; *Focus on Light* New
Jersey State Museum, Trenton; *Language to Be Looked At–Words to
Be Seen* Dwan Gallery, New York.   1968 *Language II* Dwan Gallery,
New York.   1969 *Konzeption-Conception* Städtisches Museum,
Leverkusen, West Germany.   1970 *Elements of Art* Boston Museum of
Fine Arts, Boston; *Information* The Museum of Modern Art, New
York; *Recorded Activities* Moore College of Art, Philadelphia.   1971
Artist's Video Finch College Museum of Art, New York; *Biennale*
Paris; *Body Art* John Gibson Gallery, New York; *Pier 18* The Museum
of Modern Art, New York; *Prospect '71: Projection* Kunsthalle, Düs-
seldorf; *Sonsbeek '71* Arnhem, The Netherlands; *Systems Art* Museo
de Arte Moderno, Buenos Aires.   1974 *Art/Video Confrontation 74*
Musée d'Art Moderne de la Ville de Paris, Paris; *New Aquisitions*, Tate
Gallery, London; *Project '74* Cologne; *Returned to Sender* Galleria
Schema, Florence.

Sakumi Hagiwara   Born 1946 in Tokyo. 1969 Stage Director for
Tenjo Sajiki Experimental Theater and Juzaburo Tsujimura Puppet
Company, Tokyo. 1972 Published *The Red Bicycle,* a collection of
essays. 1973 Visited the United States at invitation of U.S. State Department, Office of Educational and Cultural Affairs to see experimental film and videotape. 1974 Published *To Where? One Asks,* a collection of essays. Lives in Tokyo.   **Selected Performances**   1969 *International Experimental Theater Festival* Frankfurt.   **Selected Exhibitions and Film Showings**   1972 *Video Week* American Center, Tokyo.
1973 Tenjo Sajiki Theater Underground Cinemateque, Tokyo. 1974
Tokyo–New York Video Express Tenjo-Sajiki-Kan, Tokyo; Millennium, New York; *New Film Showcase* Underground Cinemateque,
Tokyo.

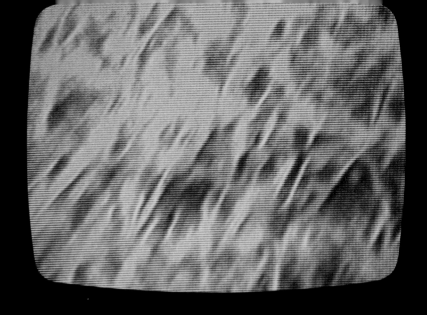

Martha Haslanger   Born 1947 in Dearborn, Michigan. BA in German Literature 1969 Denison University, Granville, Ohio. MFA 1974 Eastern Michigan University, Ypsilanti, Michigan. Awarded a grant 1974 by The Royal Film Archive of Belgium. Lives in Cambridge, Massachusetts.   **Selected Group Exhibitions**   1972 *Photography '72* Toledo Museum of Art, Toledo, Ohio; *Attitudes and Directions* Sill Gallery, Eastern Michigan University, Ypsilanti, Michigan; Mind and Sight Gallery, Toronto.   1974 Sill Gallery, Eastern Michigan University, Ypsilanti, Michigan; University of Michigan, Ann Arbor, Michigan.   **Film Festivals**   1973 *Ann Arbor Film Festival* Ann Arbor, Michigan.   1974 *Women in the Reel World* Ann Arbor, Michigan; *Ann Arbor Film Festival* Ann Arbor, Michigan (Focus prize); *Kenyon Film Festival* Kenyon College, Gambier, Ohio; *EXPRMNTL5* Fifth International Experimental Film Competition, The Royal Film Archive of Belgium, Knokke-Heist, Belgium.

Michael Hayden   Born 1943 in Vancouver, British Columbia. Attended the University of Toronto.   1967-69 A partner in Intersystems with architect Dik Zander, poet Blake Parker, and composer John Mills-Cockell. Lives in Toronto.   **Selected Exhibitions**   1966 *Presentations by Hayden* Gallery Moos, Toronto.   1967 *Sculpture '67* Nathan Phillips Square, Toronto; *Who, What, Where, Why, When* Martha Jackson Gallery, New York.   1968 *Packaging a Plan for Better Living* (with Intersystems) Gallery Moos, Toronto; *Hayden/Lajeunie* National Gallery of Canada, Ottawa; *Plastics* Art Gallery of Ontario, Toronto; *Mind Excursion Centre* Montreal; *Canadian Artists '68* Art Gallery of Ontario, Toronto.   1969 *Invasion of the Kwakamogurz* Carnegie-Mellon University, Pittsburgh; *Electric Art* Art Gallery, University of California, Los Angeles; *Art for Architecture-The Wall* Art Gallery of Ontario, Toronto.   1970 *Creative Catering* Vanier College, York University, Toronto; *Monuments '70* Hart House, University of Toronto, Toronto; *Brain Waves* Howard Wise Gallery, New York; *New Group of Seven* Electric Gallery, Toronto; *Kinetics* The Hayward Gallery, London; *Sensory Perception* Art Gallery of Ontario, Toronto.   1971 *Dive* Galerie Denis René / Hans Meyer, Düsseldorf. 1972 *Signs and Symbols* Art Gallery of Ontario, Toronto.   1973 *The Electric Show* New Brunswick Museum, St. John, New Brunswick. 1974 *Videospace* Art Gallery of Ontario, Toronto; *Project '74* Cologne.

K. H. Hödicke   Born 1938 in Nurenberg, West Germany. Studied at the Hochschule für Bildende Künster, Berlin. 1966 Lived in New York. 1967 Received Villa Massimo Prize, Rome. Lives in Berlin. **Selected Individual Exhibitions**   1965 Galerie René Block, Berlin. 1969 Galerie René Block, Berlin.   1972 Galerie René Block, Berlin.

Nancy Holt   Born in Worcester, Massachusetts. BS Jackson College, Tufts University, Medford, Massachusetts. Lives in New York. **Selected Individual Exhibitions**   1972 Art Gallery, University of Montana, Missoula, Montana; University of Rhode Island, Kingston, Rhode Island.   1973 LoGuidice Gallery, New York.   1974 Bykert Gallery, New York; Walter Kelly Gallery, Chicago.   **Selected Group Exhibitions**   1972 *5 Artists* John Weber Gallery, New York; *Work Space* 10 Bleeker Street, New York; *Encuentros* Pamplona, Spain; *6 Artists* John Weber Gallery, New York.   1973 *Women Filmmakers* The New York Cultural Center, New York; *Circuit: A Video Invitational* Everson Museum of Art, Syracuse, New York; *Art in Evolution* Xerox Square Center, Rochester, New York; *c.7,500* California Institute of the Arts, Valencia, California.   1974 *Interventions in the Landscape* Hayden Gallery, Massachusetts Institute of Technology, Cambridge, Massachusetts; *Video* Leo Castelli Gallery, New York; *Film* Sonnabend Gallery, New York; *Art Now '74* John F. Kennedy Center for the Performing Arts, Washington, D.C.; *Collectors' Video* Los Angeles County Museum of Art, Los Angeles; *Painting and Sculpture Today 1974* Indianapolis, Indiana; The Clocktower, New York; *Project '74* Cologne; *Art/Video Confrontation 74* Musée d'Art Moderne de la Ville de Paris, Paris; Artpark, Lewiston, New York.

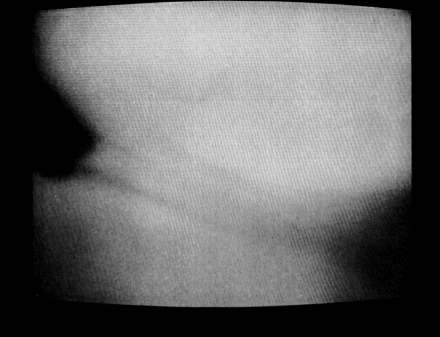

Rebecca Horn Born 1944 in Germany. Studied at Academy of Art, Hamburg. Attended 1971-72 St. Martin's School, London with DAAD grant. 1972 to present, work on films. Lives in Berlin and New York. **Selected Exhibitions** 1972 *Documenta 5* Kassel, West Germany. 1973 Galerie René Block, Berlin. 1974 *Project '74* Cologne; *Project Video* The Museum of Modern Art, New York; Palais des Beaux-Arts, Brussels.

Mako Idemitsu Born 1940 in Tokyo. Graduated 1962 Waseda University, Tokyo. 1965-73 Lived in Los Angeles. Lives in Tokyo. **Selected Individual Exhibitions** 1974 Nirenoki Gallery, Tokyo; Tenjo-Sajiki-Kan, Tokyo. **Selected Group Exhibitions and Film Showings** 1973 Womanspace, Los Angeles; *Egg and Eve Film Show* Tokyo. 1974 *Tokyo–New York Video Express* Tenjo-Sajiki-Kan, Tokyo; *100 Feet Film Festival* Sabo-Kaikan Hall, Tokyo; *New Film Showcase* Underground Cinemateque, Tokyo.

 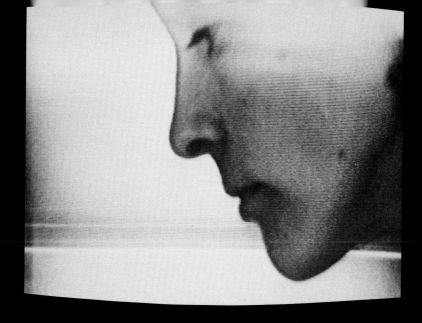

Taka Iimura Born 1937 in Tokyo. Lives in New York. **Selected Individual Film Showings** 1965 Sogetsu Cinematheque, Tokyo. 1966 Filmmakers' Cinematheque, New York. 1967 Underground Film Center, Montreal. 1968 Canyon Cinematheque, San Francisco. 1969 Institute of Contemporary Arts, London; American Center, Paris; Nederlands Filmmuseum, Amsterdam; Swedish Film Institute, Stockholm; Finish Film Archives, Helsinki; *Oberhausen Film Festival* Oberhausen, West Germany. 1970 Scorpio Theater, Tokyo. 1971 Pacific Film Archives, San Francisco. 1972 Millennium, New York; The Kitchen, New York. 1973 Der Freunde der Deutschen Kinemathek, Berlin. 1974 Cinémathèque Française, Paris. **Selected Group Exhibitions and Film Showings** 1965 *Hal House Film Festival*, Chicago. 1966 *Japanese Experimental Films* The Museum of Modern Art, New York. 1967 *The North American Film Festival* Toronto. 1968 *The Independent Film Festival* New York. 1971 *The Mainichi Contemporary Art Exhibition* Tokyo Metropolitan Art Museum, Tokyo. 1972 *St. Jude Video Invitational* de Saisset Art Gallery and Museum, University of Santa Clara, Santa Clara, California. 1973 *Circuit: A Video Invitational* Everson Museum of Art, Syracuse, New York; *Action of the Avant Garde* Akademie der Kunste, Berlin. 1974 *Project '74* Cologne; *Edinburgh Film Festival* Edinburgh; *Art/Video Confrontation 74* Musée D'Art Moderne de la Ville de Paris, Paris; *EXPRMNTL5, Fifth International Experimental Film Competition* The Royal Film Archive of Belgium, Knokke-Heist, Belgium.

Joan Jonas Born in New York. BA Mount Holyoke College, South Hadley, Massachusetts. Attended Boston Museum School, Boston. MFA Columbia University, New York. Studied dance with Tricia Brown. Lives in New York. **Individual Dance Concerts** 1970 *Underneath* Studio of Alan Saret, New York; *Mirror Check* 19th Street YMHA, New York; University of California, San Diego; *Sound Delay* Jones Beach, New York. 1971 *Overhead* Cape Breton, Nova Scotia. 1972 *Organic Honey's Visual Telepathy* LoGuidice Gallery, New York, L'Attico, Rome, and San Francisco Art Institute, San Francisco; *Delay, Delay* along the Tiber, Rome; *Documenta 5* Kassel, West Germany. 1973 *Organic Honey's Vertical Roll* Leo Castelli Gallery, New York and Festival d'Automne, Paris; *Funnel* at *Contemporanea* Rome. 1974 *Organic Honey's Vertical Roll* Boston Museum of Fine Arts, Boston; *Funnel* The Kitchen, New York and University of Massachusetts, Amherst, Massachusetts; *Crepusculo* Galleria Schema, Florence; *Project '74* Cologne; *Tunnel* Walker Art Center, Minneapolis, Minnesota. **Selected Film and Videotape Showings** 1973 *Films* Leo Castelli Gallery, New York. 1974 *Films by Artists* Film Forum, New York. 1975 Anthology Film Archives, New York; *Americans in Florence: Europeans in Florence* Long Beach Museum of Art, Long Beach, California.

Allan Kaprow   Born 1927 in Atlantic City, New Jersey. Studied painting 1947-48 Hans Hofmann School of Fine Arts, New York. BA 1949 New York University, New York. MA in History of Art 1952 Columbia University, New York. Lives in Pasadena, California. **Selected Individual Exhibitions**   1953 Hansa Gallery, New York. 1959 Reuben Gallery, New York. 1967 Pasadena Museum of Art, Pasadena, California. 1974 *Live* Stefanotty Gallery, New York. **Selected Group Exhibitions**   1957 *The New York School: Second Generation* The Jewish Museum, New York. 1958 *Pittsburgh International Exhibit of Contemporary Painting and Sculpture* Carnegie Institute, Pittsburgh. 1959 *Art Out of the Ordinary* Contemporary Arts Museum, Houston, Texas. 1960 *New Media, New Forms, Version I* Martha Jackson Gallery, New York. 1967 *Pictures to Be Read, Poetry to Be Seen* Museum of Contemporary Art, Chicago. 1969 *Work* The Jewish Museum, New York. 1970 *Happening & Fluxus* Kunstverein, Cologne. 1974 *Contemporanea* Rome; *Project '74* Cologne. **Selected Happenings and Events**   1958 *A Concert of New Music, Sound Piece* The Living Theatre, New York. 1960 *Coca-Cola, Shirley Cannonball?* Judson Hall, New York. 1961 *Art in Motion* Stedelijk Museum, Amsterdam. 1962 *Chicken* YM/YWHA, Philadelphia. 1964 *Avant-Garde Festival* New York. 1970 *Tag* Aspen Design Conference, Aspen, Colorado. 1973 *Basic Thermal Units* Volkswang Museum, Essen, West Germany. 1974 *2nd Routine* Stefanotty Gallery, New York. **Broadcasts**   1967 "Watching" in *Gateway to the Arts* WCBS-TV New York. 1969 *Hello* WGBH-TV Boston.

Nobuhiro Kawanaka   Born 1941 in Tokyo. 1960 Started filmmaking and organized *Eight Generation,* a film group in Tokyo. 1968 Joined Japan Filmmakers Cooperative, Tokyo. 1969 Founded Japan Underground Center, Tokyo. Lives in Tokyo. **Individual Exhibitions**   1972 Tenjo-Sajiki-Kan, Tokyo. 1974 Tenjo-Sajiki-Kan, Tokyo. **Selected Group Exhibitions**   1971 *Global Art Vision '71* Korakuen Hall, Tokyo. 1972 *Do-It-Yourself-Video-Kit/Video Communication* Sony Building, Tokyo; *Catastrophe Art* San Fedele Gallery, Milan; *Video Week* American Center, Tokyo. 1974 *Tokyo–New York Video Express* Tenjo-Sajiki-Kan, Tokyo; *Up Art Communication* German Culture Center, Tokyo; *New Music Media Festival* Karuizawa; *The Video Game Festival* Karuizawa. **Selected Film Showings**   1966 *Art Festival Shinjuku* Art Theater, Tokyo. 1968 *The First Film Ceremony* Sasori-za, Tokyo. 1969 *Intermedia Art Festival* Nikkei Hall, Tokyo; *The Fourth Film Ceremony* Theater 36, Nagoya; *The Fifth Film Ceremony* Meiji-Seimei Hall, Fukuoka; *The Sixth Film Ceremony* Ikebukuro Art Theater, Tokyo. 1970 Momoyama-Gakuin University, Osaka; Kyoto University, Kyoto. 1972 Mozart Salon, Tokyo; Munich City Theater, Munich. 1973 *Video Symposium with Hans Magnus Enzenberger* Tokyo; Kinokuniya Hall, Tokyo; Yasuda-Seimei Hall, Tokyo; Espace Giraux, Tokyo; *International Film Festival* Pessaro, Italy; Italian Cultural Center, Tokyo. 1974 Millennium, New York; Film Forum, New York; *100 Feet Film Festival* Sabo-kaikan Hall, Tokyo; American Center, Tokyo.

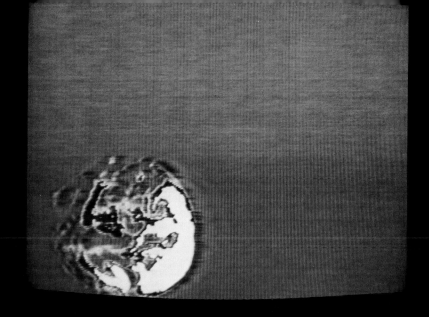

Hakudo Kobayashi   Born 1944 in Sendai, Japan. Graduated 1967 Tama Fine Arts University, Tokyo.   1967-70 Made Hakudo machines. Lives in Tokyo.   **Selected Group Exhibitions**   1972 *Video Communication Art* Core Hall, Kyoto; *Video Week* American Center, Tokyo. 1973 *Hello Video Show* Tokyo.   1974 *Tokyo Biennial '74* Tokyo Metropolitan Art Museum, Tokyo; *The Video Game Festival* Karuizawa; *Le Salon Video* Geneva; *The Japan Art Festival* Musée d'Art Contemporain, Montreal and The Vancouver Art Gallery, Vancouver, British Columbia.

Masao Komura   Born 1943 in Tokyo. Graduated 1966 Tama Fine Arts University, Tokyo. 1966 Founded Computer Technique Group. 1968 Organized Design Studio M. 1969 Dissolved Computer Technique Group. 1970 Established Institute of Image Engineering. 1972 Organized Computer Art Center, Tokyo. Lives in Tokyo. **Selected Group Exhibitions**   1968 *Cybernetic Serendipity* Institute of Contemporary Arts, London, The Corcoran Gallery of Art, Washington, D.C.   1970 *Biennale* Paris.   1972 *Video Week* American Center, Tokyo.   1973 *Computer Art '73/Cybernetic Art Trip* Tokyo. 1974 *Tokyo Biennial '74* Tokyo Metropolitan Art Museum, Tokyo; *Computer Art '74* Tokyo.

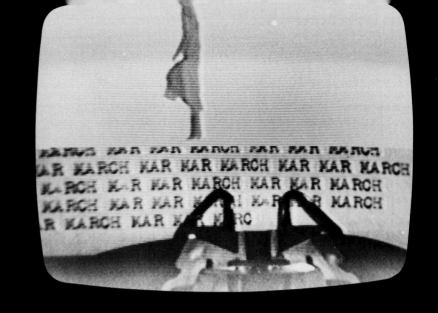

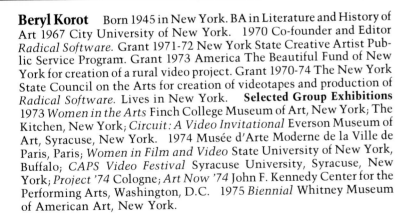

Beryl Korot   Born 1945 in New York. BA in Literature and History of Art 1967 City University of New York.   1970 Co-founder and Editor *Radical Software*. Grant 1971-72 New York State Creative Artist Public Service Program. Grant 1973 America The Beautiful Fund of New York for creation of a rural video project. Grant 1970-74 The New York State Council on the Arts for creation of videotapes and production of *Radical Software*. Lives in New York.   **Selected Group Exhibitions** 1973 *Women in the Arts* Finch College Museum of Art, New York; The Kitchen, New York; *Circuit: A Video Invitational* Everson Museum of Art, Syracuse, New York.   1974 Musée d'Arte Moderne de la Ville de Paris, Paris; *Women in Film and Video* State University of New York, Buffalo; *CAPS Video Festival* Syracuse University, Syracuse, New York; *Project '74* Cologne; *Art Now '74* John F. Kennedy Center for the Performing Arts, Washington, D.C.   1975 *Biennial* Whitney Museum of American Art, New York.

Paul Kos   Born 1942 in Rock Springs, Wyoming. Attended Georgetown University, Washington, D.C. BFA 1965 San Francisco Art Institute, San Francisco. MFA 1967 San Francisco Art Institute. Lives in San Francisco.   **Selected Individual Exhibitions**   1969 *Participation-kinetics* Richmond Art Center, Richmond, California. 1971 Reese Palley Gallery, New York.   1974 M.H. de Young Museum, San Francisco.   **Selected Group Exhibitions**   1970 *Art in the Mind* Allen Memorial Art Museum, Oberlin College, Oberlin, Ohio; *The Eighties* University Art Museum, University of California, Berkeley. 1971 *Fish, Fox, Kos* de Saisset Art Gallery and Museum, University of Santa Clara, Santa Clara, California; *Video Works* 112 Greene Street, New York.   1972 *St. Jude Video Invitational* de Saisset Art Gallery and Museum, University of Santa Clara, Santa Clara, California; *San Francisco Performance* Newport Harbor Art Museum, Newport Beach, California; *San Francisco Video Artists* Tacoma Art Museum, Tacoma, Washington; *Video West One* Everson Museum of Art, Syracuse, New York.   1973 *Bienal* São Paulo; *Circuit: A Video Invitational* Everson Museum of Art, Syracuse, New York; *Guterrez-Solana, Glassman, Kos* La Jolla Museum of Art, La Jolla, California; *Video Group Show* Leo Castelli Gallery, New York.   1974 *Art Now '74* John F. Kennedy Center for the Performing Arts, Washington, D.C.; *Collectors' Video* Los Angeles County Museum of Art, Los Angeles; *Contemporanea* Rome; *Trigon '74* Neue Galerie am Landesmuseum Joanneum, Graz, Austria; *Project '74* Cologne.   **Broadcast** 1974 *Video: The New Wave* produced by WGBH-TV Boston.

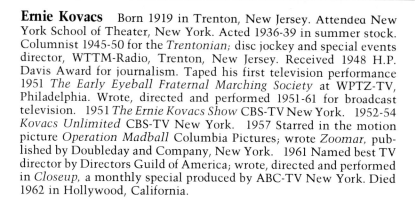

Ernie Kovacs   Born 1919 in Trenton, New Jersey. Attended New York School of Theater, New York. Acted 1936-39 in summer stock. Columnist 1945-50 for the *Trentonian*; disc jockey and special events director, WTTM-Radio, Trenton, New Jersey. Received 1948 H.P. Davis Award for journalism. Taped his first television performance 1951 *The Early Eyeball Fraternal Marching Society* at WPTZ-TV, Philadelphia. Wrote, directed and performed 1951-61 for broadcast television. 1951 *The Ernie Kovacs Show* CBS-TV New York. 1952-54 *Kovacs Unlimited* CBS-TV New York. 1957 Starred in the motion picture *Operation Madball* Columbia Pictures; wrote *Zoomar*, published by Doubleday and Company, New York. 1961 Named best TV director by Directors Guild of America; wrote, directed and performed in *Closeup*, a monthly special produced by ABC-TV New York. Died 1962 in Hollywood, California.

Shigeko Kubota   Born in Niigata, Japan. BA in Sculpture 1963 Tokyo University, Tokyo. Graduate study 1963-66 New York University, New York, New School for Social Research, New York, and Art School of The Brooklyn Museum, Brooklyn, New York. Appointed 1964 Vice-Chairman, Fluxus, New York. Lives in New York. **Selected Individual Exhibitions**   1964 *Make a Floor of Love Letters* Naiqua Gallery, Tokyo. 1972 *Video Birthday Party for John Cage* The Kitchen, New York; Everson Museum of Art, Syracuse, New York. 1973 *Wabash Transit* School of The Art Institute of Chicago, Chicago.   **Selected Group Exhibitions**   1962 *Yomiuri Shinbun Independent Exhibition* Tokyo Municipal Museum, Tokyo. 1972 *1st Annual Video Festival* The Kitchen, New York; *1st Annual Women's Video Festival* The Kitchen, New York; *Yellow, Black, White and Red* The Kitchen, New York; *St. Jude Video Invitational* de Saisset Art Gallery and Museum, University of Santa Clara, Santa Clara, California. *Video Exhibition* Wesleyan University, Middletown, Connecticut. 1973 *2nd Annual Video Festival* The Kitchen, New York; *Women's International Film Festival* Toronto; *Women's Video Festival* University of Illinois, Chicago; *Circuit: A Video Invitational* Everson Museum of Art, Syracuse, New York. 1974 *Women in Film and Video* State University of New York, Buffalo; *Open Circuits: The Future of Television* The Museum of Modern Art, New York; *Video Celebration for John Cage* Harvard University, Cambridge, Massachusetts; *Tokyo–New York Video Express* Tenjo-Sajiki-Kan Tokyo.

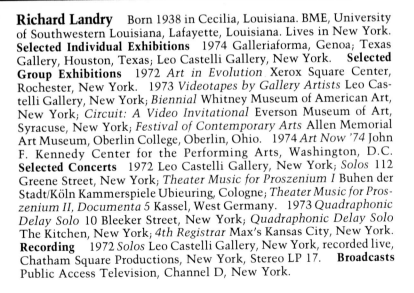

Richard Landry Born 1938 in Cecilia, Louisiana. BME, University of Southwestern Louisiana, Lafayette, Louisiana. Lives in New York. **Selected Individual Exhibitions** 1974 Galleriaforma, Genoa; Texas Gallery, Houston, Texas; Leo Castelli Gallery, New York. **Selected Group Exhibitions** 1972 *Art in Evolution* Xerox Square Center, Rochester, New York. 1973 *Videotapes by Gallery Artists* Leo Castelli Gallery, New York; *Biennial* Whitney Museum of American Art, New York; *Circuit: A Video Invitational* Everson Museum of Art, Syracuse, New York; *Festival of Contemporary Arts* Allen Memorial Art Museum, Oberlin College, Oberlin, Ohio. 1974 *Art Now '74* John F. Kennedy Center for the Performing Arts, Washington, D.C. **Selected Concerts** 1972 Leo Castelli Gallery, New York; *Solos* 112 Greene Street, New York; *Theater Music for Proszenium I* Buhen der Stadt/Köln Kammerspiele Ubieuring, Cologne; *Theater Music for Proszenium II, Documenta 5* Kassel, West Germany. 1973 *Quadraphonic Delay Solo* 10 Bleeker Street, New York; *Quadraphonic Delay Solo* The Kitchen, New York; *4th Registrar* Max's Kansas City, New York. **Recording** 1972 *Solos* Leo Castelli Gallery, New York, recorded live, Chatham Square Productions, New York, Stereo LP 17. **Broadcasts** Public Access Television, Channel D, New York.

Les Levine Born 1936 in Dublin, Ireland. Educated 1953-57 Central School of Arts and Crafts, London. Emigrated 1958 to Canada. Lives in New York. **Selected Individual Exhibitions** 1965 The Isaacs Gallery, Toronto. 1966 Fischbach Gallery, New York. 1967 Walker Art Center, Minneapolis, Minnesota; The Museum of Modern Art, New York. 1970 *New Branch in Bremen* Galerie de Gestlo, Bremen, West Germany. 1972 *The Troubles: An Artist's Document of Ulster* Finch College Museum of Art, New York. 1974 *Language ÷ Emotion + Syntax = Message* The Vancouver Art Gallery, Vancouver, British Columbia. **Selected Group Exhibitions** 1965 *6th Biennial of Canadian Sculpture* National Gallery of Canada, Ottawa. 1966 *The Object Transformed* The Museum of Modern Art, New York. 1967 *Dada, Surrealism and Today* The Museum of Modern Art, New York; *Canada '67* Canadian Government Exhibition Commission, Union Carbide Building, New York; *Schemata 7* Finch College Museum of Art, New York. 1969 *Vision and Television* Rose Art Museum, Brandeis University, Waltham, Massachusetts; *Plastics Presence* The Jewish Museum, New York; *Bienal* São Paulo; *Between Object and Environment* Institute of Contemporary Art, University of Pennsylvania, Philadelphia; *Annual* Whitney Museum of American Art, New York. 1970 *Monumental Art* Cincinnati Museum, Cincinnati, Ohio; *Recorded Activities* Moore College of Art, Philadelphia; *Software Show* The Jewish Museum, New York; *Information* The Museum of Modern Art, New York; *Art in the Mind* Allen Memorial Art Museum, Oberlin College, Oberlin, Ohio. 1974 *Live* Stefanotty Gallery, New York; *Project '74* Cologne.

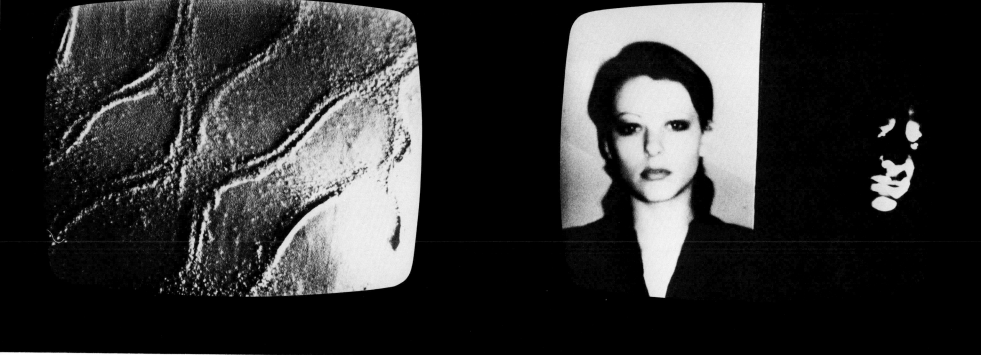

Alvin Lucier Born 1931 in Nashua, New Hampshire. Studied music with Howard Boatwright, David Kraehenbuhl and Quincy Porter at Yale University, New Haven, Connecticut; Arthur Berger, Irving Fine and Harold Shapero at Brandeis University, Waltham, Massachusetts; Lukas Foss at Tanglewood, Lenox, Massachusetts. Received a Fulbright-Hayes Fellowship to Rome to study with Boris Porena. 1961 Met Frederic Rzewski and David Tudor. 1962 Director of Brandeis Choral Union. 1964 Founded Sonic Arts Union with Robert Ashley, David Behrman and Gordon Mumma. 1970 to the present, Director of Electronic and Computer Music Facility, Wesleyan University, Middletown, Connecticut. 1973 to the present, Musical Director of the Viola Farber Dance Company. Lives in Middletown, Connecticut. **Principal Compositions** 1962 *Action Music for Piano; Song for Soprano.* 1965 *Music for Solo Performer.* 1967 *North American Time Capsule; Vespers.* 1968 *Chambers.* 1969 *The Only Talking Machine in the World.* 1970 *Hartford Memory Space; I Am Sitting in a Room; Quasimodo, The Great Lover.* 1971 *The Duke of York; Gentle Fire.* 1972 *The Queen of the South; Room Stimulation 1; The Bird of Bremen Flies Through the Houses of the Burghers.* **Compositions for the Theater** 1965 John Arden's *The Waters of Babylon* Brandeis University, Waltham, Massachusetts. 1969 William Shakespeare's *King Henry V* American Shakespeare Festival, Stratford, Connecticut.

Urs Lüthi Born 1947 in Lucerne, Switzerland. Lives in Zürich and Milan. **Selected Individual Exhibitions** 1966 Galerie Beat Mäder, Bern, Switzerland. 1969 Galerie Junge Generation, Hamburg; Kabinett für aktuelle Kunst, Bremerhaven, West Germany. 1970 Galerie Toni Gerber, Bern, Switzerland. 1972 Galleria Diagramma, Milan. 1973 Galleria Conz, Venice; Galerie Krinzinger, Innsbruck, Austria; Galleria Rumma, Naples; Galerie Nächst St. Stephan, Vienna. 1974 Galerie Impact, Lausanne; Kunstmuseum, Lucerne; Neue Galerie am Landesmuseum Joanneum, Graz, Austria. **Selected Group Exhibitions** 1968 Neue Galerie, am Landesmuseum Joanneum, Graz, Austria; *22 Young Swiss* Stedelijk Museum, Amsterdam; *Plans and Project in Art* Kunsthalle, Bern, Switzerland. 1971 *Swiss Avant Garde* The New York Cultural Center, New York; *Biennale* Paris; Musée d'Arte Moderne, Lausanne. 1972 *Young Swiss Art* Rotunda della Besana, Milan; *Profile X* Kunstmuseum, Bochum, West Germany. 1973 *Contemporanea* Rome; *Trigon '73* Neue Galerie am Landesmuseum Joanneum, Graz, Austria. 1974 *Ambient '74* Kunstmuseum, Winterthur, Switzerland; *Project '74* Cologne; 1975 *Americans in Florence: Europeans in Florence* Long Beach Museum of Art, Long Beach, California.

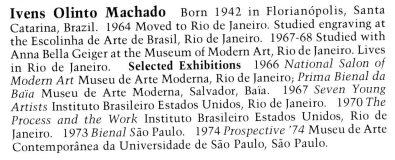

Ivens Olinto Machado   Born 1942 in Florianópolis, Santa Catarina, Brazil. 1964 Moved to Rio de Janeiro. Studied engraving at the Escolinha de Arte de Brasil, Rio de Janeiro. 1967-68 Studied with Anna Bella Geiger at the Museum of Modern Art, Rio de Janeiro. Lives in Rio de Janeiro.   **Selected Exhibitions**   1966 *National Salon of Modern Art* Museu de Arte Moderna, Rio de Janeiro; *Prima Bienal da Baïa* Museu de Arte Moderna, Salvador, Baïa.   1967 *Seven Young Artists* Instituto Brasileiro Estados Unidos, Rio de Janeiro.   1970 *The Process and the Work* Instituto Brasileiro Estados Unidos, Rio de Janeiro.   1973 *Bienal* São Paulo.   1974 *Prospective '74* Museu de Arte Contemporânea da Universidade de São Paulo, São Paulo.

Andy Mann   Born 1947 in New York. United States Navy 1965-69. BA 1973 New York University, New York. Lives in New York. **Selected Group Exhibitions**   1972 The Kitchen, New York.   1973 *Bienal* São Paulo; *Trigon '73* Neue Galerie am Landesmuseum Joanneum, Graz, Austria; The Kitchen, New York; *Circuit: A Video Invitational* Everson Museum of Art, Syracuse, New York.   1974 *Collectors' Video* Los Angeles County Museum of Art, Los Angeles; *Art Now '74* John F. Kennedy Center for the Performing Arts, Washington, D.C.; *Project '74* Cologne.

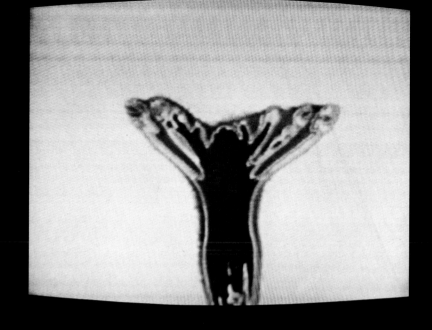

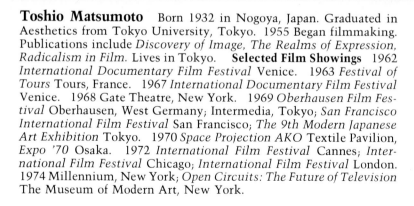

Toshio Matsumoto Born 1932 in Nogoya, Japan. Graduated in Aesthetics from Tokyo University, Tokyo. 1955 Began filmmaking. Publications include *Discovery of Image, The Realms of Expression, Radicalism in Film.* Lives in Tokyo. **Selected Film Showings** 1962 *International Documentary Film Festival* Venice. 1963 *Festival of Tours* Tours, France. 1967 *International Documentary Film Festival* Venice. 1968 Gate Theatre, New York. 1969 *Oberhausen Film Festival* Oberhausen, West Germany; Intermedia, Tokyo; *San Francisco International Film Festival* San Francisco; *The 9th Modern Japanese Art Exhibition* Tokyo. 1970 *Space Projection AKO* Textile Pavilion, Expo '70 Osaka. 1972 *International Film Festival* Cannes; *International Film Festival* Chicago; *International Film Festival* London. 1974 Millennium, New York; *Open Circuits: The Future of Television* The Museum of Modern Art, New York.

Kyoko Michishita Born in Japan. BA in Journalism 1967 University of Wisconsin, Madison, Wisconsin. 1967-69 Guide at United Nations Headquarters, New York. 1969 Assistant to *Christian Science Monitor* correspondent, Tokyo. Press Assistant 1970-71 United States Pavillion, *Expo '70* Osaka. 1971 to the present, Program Director, American Center, Tokyo. Lives in Tokyo.

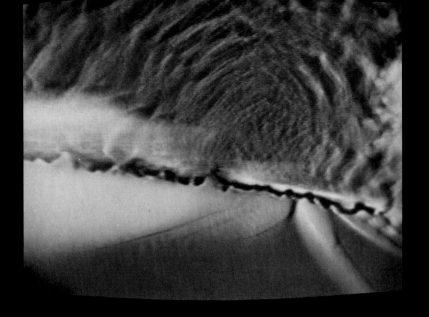

Robert Morris   Born 1931 in Kansas City, Missouri. Studied 1948-50 University of Kansas City and Kansas City Art Institute, Kansas City, Missouri. 1951 California School of Fine Arts, San Francisco 1953-54 Reed College, Portland, Oregon. Graduate study 1961-62 Hunter College, New York. Lives in New York.   **Selected Individual Exhibitions** 1957   Dilexi Gallery, San Francisco.   1963 Green Gallery, New York. 1964 Galerie Schmela, Düsseldorf.   1966 Dwan Gallery, New York.   1967 Leo Castelli Gallery, New York.   1968 Stedelijk van Abbemuseum, Eindhoven, The Netherlands.   1969 The Corcoran Gallery of Art, Washington, D.C.   1970 The Detroit Institute of Arts, Detroit; Whitney Museum of American Art, New York.   1971 Tate Gallery, London.   1974 Institute of Contemporary Art, University of Pennsylvania, Philadelphia.   **Selected Group Exhibitions** 1963 *Black, White & Gray* Wadsworth Atheneum, Hartford, Connecticut.   1966 *Art in Progress* Finch College Museum of Art, New York; *Annual* Whitney Museum of American Art, New York.   1967 *American Sculpture of the Sixties* Los Angeles County Museum, Los Angeles.   1969 *Square Pegs in Round Holes* Stedelijk Museum, Amsterdam; *Anti-Illusion: Procedures/Materials* Whitney Museum of American Art, New York; *Art by Telephone* Museum of Contemporary Art, Chicago.   1970 *Information* The Museum of Modern Art, New York; *Monumental Art* Contemporary Arts Center, Cincinnati   1971 *Prospect '71: Projection* Kunsthalle, Düsseldorf; *Works for New Spaces* Walker Art Center, Minneapolis.   1973 *Biennial* Whitney Museum of American Art, New York; *Project '74* Cologne.

Philip Morton   Born 1945 in Sandy Lake, Pennsylvania. BA in Art Education 1967 Pennsylvania State University, University Park, Pennsylvania. MA in Art 1968 Purdue University, Lafayette, Indiana.   1969 Began developing an experimental video program and later established *Video Data Bank* at School of Art Institute of Chicago, Chicago.   1974 Established P-Pis, or Pied-Piper Interactioning-System, a cable TV station, South Haven, Michigan. Lives in Chicago. **Selected Exhibitions and Performances**   1969 *Southeast and Texas Biennial* Isaac Delgado Museum, New Orleans, Louisiana.   1970 *Film/Video Ritual* Chicago; Isaac Delgado Museum, New Orleans, Louisiana.   1972 *Videopolis* University of Illinois, Circle Campus, Chicago.   1973 *In Consecration of New Space,* an event utilizing the Sandin Image Processor and the Paik-Abe Video Synthesizer, University of Illinois, Circle Campus, Chicago. *Beating Love* School of Art Institute of Chicago, Chicago.   1974 *Terminus-Imirage* Chicago.

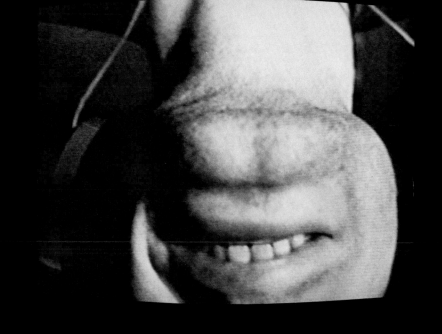

Fujiko Nakaya Born 1938 in Sapporo, Japan. Graduated from Northwestern University, Evanston, Illinois. 1969 Joined Experiments in Art and Technology and opened EAT office in Tokyo. 1970 Designed fog sculpture for the Pepsi-Cola Pavilion, *Expo '70* Osaka. 1971 Collaborated with EAT, New York, The Moderna Museet, Stockholm and The National Institute of Design, Ahmedabad, India for information sculpture *Utopia Q & A 1981.* 1972 Joined Video Hiroba. 1973 Researcher for City Redevelopment Program, Yokohama. 1974 Translated *Guerrilla Television* by Michael Shamberg into Japanese and worked on video community project for Niigata City. Lives in Tokyo. **Selected Group Exhibitions and Film Showings** 1972 *Do-It-Yourself Kit/Video Communication* Sony Building, Tokyo; *Video Week* American Center, Tokyo. 1973 *Matrix International Video Conference* Vancouver, British Columbia; *Women's Video Festival* Toronto; *International Film Festival* Pessaro, Italy; *Equivalent Cinema '73* Municipal Museum of Fine Arts, Kyoto; *Computer Art '73* Tokyo. 1974 *Tokyo–New York Video Express* Tenjo-Sajiki-Kan, Tokyo; *Tokyo Biennial* Tokyo Metropolitan Art Museum, Tokyo; Gallery Signum, Kyoto; *The Video-Game Festival* Karuizawa.

Bruce Nauman Born 1941 in Fort Wayne, Indiana. BS 1964 University of Wisconsin, Madison. MA 1966 University of California, Davis. Lives in Altadena, California. **Selected Individual Exhibitions** 1966 Nicholas Wilder Gallery, Los Angeles. 1968 Leo Castelli Gallery, New York. 1971 Stedelijk van Abbemuseum, Einhoven, The Netherlands. 1973 Los Angeles County Museum of Art, Los Angeles; Whitney Museum of American Art, New York; Kunsthalle, Düsseldorf. **Selected Group Exhibitions** 1967 *American Sculpture of the Sixties* Los Angeles County Museum of Art, Los Angeles. 1968 *Documenta 4* Kassel, West Germany. 1969 *Art by Telephone* Museum of Contemporary Art, Chicago; *Anti-Illusion: Procedures and Materials* Whitney Museum of American Art, New York; *Square Pegs in Round Holes* Stedelijk Museum, Amsterdam; *31st Annual Exhibition* The Corcoran Gallery of Art, Washington, D.C.; *When Attitude Becomes Form* Kunsthalle, Bern, Switzerland. 1970 *Against Order: Chance and Art* Institute of Contemporary Art, University of Pennsylvania, Philadelphia; *Annual* Whitney Museum of American Art, New York; *Information* The Museum of Modern Art, New York; *10th International Exhibition of Japan* Tokyo; *Recorded Activities* Moore College of Art, Philadelphia. 1971 *Projected Art* Finch College Museum of Art, New York; *6th Guggenheim International* The Solomon R. Guggenheim Museum, New York. 1972 *Diagrams and Drawings* The Kroller-Muller Museum, Otterlo, The Netherlands. 1973 *American Art–Third Quarter-Century* The Seattle Art Museum, Seattle, Washington. 1974 *Contemporanea* Rome; *Project '74* Cologne.

35

Dennis Oppenheim Born 1938 in Mason City, Washington. Lives in New York. **Selected Individual Exhibitions** 1968 *Ground Systems* John Gibson Gallery, New York. 1969 *A Report: Two Ocean Projects* The Museum of Modern Art, New York. 1972 *Projections* Nova Scotia College of Art and Design, Halifax, Nova Scotia; *2000' Shadow Projection* The Tate Gallery, London. 1973 Galerie Ileana Sonnabend, Paris. **Selected Group Exhibitions** 1969 *955,000* Vancouver Art Gallery, Vancouver, British Columbia; *Art After Plans* Kunsthalle, Bern, Switzerland; *Art by Telephone* Museum of Contemporary Art, Chicago; *When Attitudes Become Form* Kunsthalle, Bern, Switzerland; *Square Pegs in Round Holes* Stedelijk Museum, Amsterdam; *Land Art* Fernsehgalerie Gerry Schum, Düsseldorf; *Earth Art* Andrew Dickenson White Museum of Art, Cornell University, Ithaca, New York; *Annual* Whitney Museum of American Art, New York. 1970 *Against Order: Chance and Art* Institute of Contemporary Art, University of Pennsylvania, Philadelphia; *Conceptual Art/Arte Povera/Land Art* Galleria Civica d'Arte Moderna, Turin; *Recorded Activities* Moore College of Art, Philadelphia; *Information* The Museum of Modern Art, New York. 1971 *Biennale* Paris; *Prospect '71: Projection* Kunsthalle, Düsseldorf; *Sonsbeek '71* Arnhem, The Netherlands; *Pier 18* The Museum of Modern Art, New York. 1972 *Making Megalopolis Matter* The New York Cultural Center, New York; *Documenta 5* Kassel, West Germany. 1974 *Art Now '74* John F. Kennedy Center for the Performing Arts, Washington D.C.; *Project '74* Cologne.

Jean Otth Born 1940 in Lausanne, Switzerland. Studied history of art and philosophy of science 1959-64 University of Lausanne. Attended 1961-63 École des Beaux-Arts de Lausanne. Lived in Chicago and New York. 1971-73 Participated in an experimental course of René Berger entitled "Esthetics and Mass Media" at the University of Lausanne. Lives in Lausanne. **Selected Individual Exhibitions** 1966 Galerie Paul Fachetti, Paris. 1970 Galerie Impact, Lausanne. **Selected Group Exhibitions** 1966 Galerie de l'Entracte, Lausanne. 1971 *Le Groupe IMPACT* Musée des Beaux-Arts, Montreal. 1975 *Americans in Florence: Europeans in Florence* Long Beach Museum of Art, Long Beach, California.

Nam June Paik Born 1932 in Seoul, Korea. Graduated 1956 University of Tokyo. Studied music, art history and philosophy 1956-1958 University of Munich, Freiburg Conservatory, and University of Cologne. 1958-1961 Studio for Electronic Music of Radio Cologne. Artist in Residence 1969 WGBH-TV Boston, 1971 WNET-TV New York. Lives in New York. **Selected Individual Events** 1959 Galeria 22, Düsseldorf. 1960 Atelier Mary Bauermeister, Cologne. 1962 Kammerspiele, Düsseldorf. 1965 Bonino Gallery, New York. 1971 *Paik-Abe Video Synthesizer* Bonino Gallery, New York. 1972 *Cine-Probe* The Museum of Modern Art, New York. 1973 The Kitchen, New York. 1974 Everson Museum of Art, Syracuse, New York. **Selected Group Events** 1962 *Fluxus Festival* Museum of Wiesbaden, West Germany. 1968 *Cybernetic Serendipity* Institute of Contemporary Arts, London; *The Machine As Seen at the End of the Mechanical Age* The Museum of Modern Art, New York. 1969 *TV As a Creative Medium* Howard Wise Gallery, New York; *Vision and Television* Rose Art Museum, Brandeis University, Waltham, Massachusetts. 1971 *St. Jude Video Invitational* de Saisset Art Gallery and Museum, University of Santa Clara, Santa Clara, California. 1973 *Circuit: A Video Invitational* Everson Museum of Art, Syracuse, New York. 1974 *Open Circuits: The Future of Television* The Museum of Modern Art, New York. **Selected Broadcasts** 1969 *Medium Is the Medium* WGBH-TV Boston. 1970 *Video Commune* WGBH-TV Boston. 1972 *The Selling of New York* WNET-TV New York. 1974 *Tribute to John Cage* WNET-TV New York.

Giulio Paolini Born 1940 in Genoa, Italy. Lives in Turin. **Selected Individual Exhibitions** 1964 Galleria La Salita, Rome. 1965 Galleria Notizie, Turin. 1966 Galleria dell' Ariete, Milan. 1967 Galleria del Leone, Venice; Galleria Christian Stein, Turin; *Una Poesia* Libreria Stampatori, Turin. 1968 Libreria dell'Oca, Rome. 1969 *212 1969* Galleria De Nieubourg, Milan. 1970 *Vedo* Galleria Notizie, Turin. **Selected Group Exhibitions** 1966 *Aspetti dell'avanguardia in Italia* Galleria Notizie, Turin; *Premio San Fedele* Milan; Galleria Schwarz, Milan; *Situazioni '66* Galleria del Deposito, Turin. 1967 *Collage 1* Instituto di Storia del' Arte, Universita de Genoa, Genoa. 1968 *International Exhibition of Drawings* University of Puerto Rico, Mayaqüez, Puerto Rico. 1969 *International Festival of Painting* Cagnes-sur-Mer, France; *Biennale* Paris. 1970 *Biennale Internazionale Della Giovane Pittura* Museo Civico, Bologna; *Information* The Museum of Modern Art, New York; *Biennale* Venice; *Conceptual Art/Arte Povera/Land Art* Galleria Civica d'Arte Moderna, Turin. 1971 *Formulation* Addison Gallery of American Art, Andover, Massachusetts; *Nuovi termi di riferimento per il linguaggio artistico* Galleria d'Arte Moderna, Palazzo Pitti, Florence; *Arte Povera* Kunstverein, Munich; *Biennale* Paris. 1972 *Documenta 5* Kassel, West Germany. 1974 *Project '74* Cologne; *Americans in Florence: Europeans in Florence* Long Beach Museum of Art, Long Beach, California.

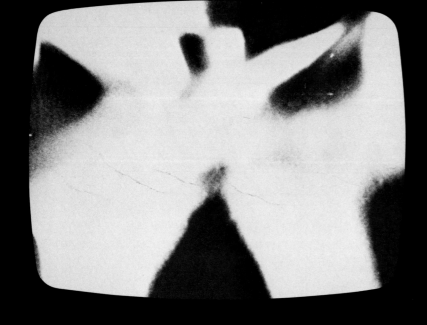 

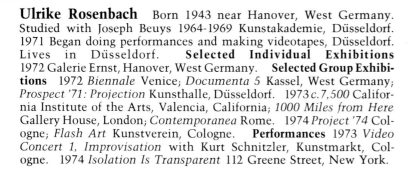

Ulrike Rosenbach   Born 1943 near Hanover, West Germany. Studied with Joseph Beuys 1964-1969 Kunstakademie, Düsseldorf. 1971 Began doing performances and making videotapes, Düsseldorf. Lives in Düsseldorf.   **Selected Individual Exhibitions** 1972 Galerie Ernst, Hanover, West Germany.   **Selected Group Exhibitions**   1972 *Biennale* Venice; *Documenta 5* Kassel, West Germany; *Prospect '71: Projection* Kunsthalle, Düsseldorf.   1973 *c. 7,500* California Institute of the Arts, Valencia, California; *1000 Miles from Here* Gallery House, London; *Contemporanea* Rome.   1974 *Project '74* Cologne; *Flash Art* Kunstverein, Cologne.   **Performances** 1973 *Video Concert 1, Improvisation* with Kurt Schnitzler, Kunstmarkt, Cologne.   1974 *Isolation Is Transparent* 112 Greene Street, New York.

Reiner Ruthenbeck   Born 1937 in Velbert, West Germany. 1962 After working as a photographer, studied with Joseph Beuys, Kunstakademie, Düsseldorf. Lives in Düsseldorf-Oberkassel. **Selected Individual Exhibitions**   1967 Galerie Konrad Fischer, Düsseldorf.   1968 Wide White Space, Antwerp.   1969 *Blockade* Galerie René Block, Berlin; Galerie Heiner Friedrich, Munich.   1970 *Identifications* Fernehgalerie, Hanover.   1971 Westfälisher Kunstverein, Munster. 1972 Städtisches Museum, Monchengladbach; Stedelijk Museum, Amsterdam.   1973 Kunstverein, Krefeld; Kunsthalle, Kiel.   1974 Galerie René Block, Berlin; Städtische Kunsthalle, Düsseldorf; Galerie Preisig, Basel, Switzerland.   **Selected Group Exhibitions**   1968 *Round Pegs in Square Holes* Stedelijk Museum, Amsterdam.   1969 *When Attitude Becomes Form* Kunsthalle, Bern, Switzerland; *Prospect '69* Kunsthalle, Düsseldorf.   1970 *Strategy: Get Arts* Edinburgh International Festival, Edinburgh.   1971 *City '71* Von-der-Heydt-Museum, Wuppertal.   1972 *Documenta 5* Kassel.   1974 *Project '74* Cologne.

Daniel Sandin   Born 1942 in Rockford, Illinois. BS in Physics 1964 Shimer College, Mount Carroll, Illinois. MS in Physics 1967 University of Wisconsin, Madison, Wisconsin. 1971-74 Designed and built the Image Processor, an analog computer. 1972-73 Developed a series of courses related to the expressive use of computers, video, and other new technologies. 1972 Co-director, *Videopolis*, University of Illinois, Circle Campus, Chicago. 1974 Created special effects for a feature film *U.F.O.–Target Earth*. Lives in Chicago.   **Selected Exhibitions and Performances**   1969 *Glow-Flow* University of Wisconsin, Madison, Wisconsin.   1971 *Yohara I* Smithsonian Institute, Washington, D.C.; *Video Interactive Environment* Evanston Art Center, Evanston, Illinois.   1973 *In Consecration of New Space*, an event utilizing the Sandin Image Processor and the Paik-Abe Synthesizer, University of Illinois, Circle Campus, Chicago; *Video Data Bank* School of The Art Institute of Chicago, Chicago.   1974 *Open Circuits: The Future of Television* The Museum of Modern Art, New York.   **Selected Broadcasts**   1973 *Future Shock* WTTW-TV Chicago.   1974 *Video–the New Wave* WGBH-TV, Boston.

Ira Schneider   Born 1939 in New York. BA 1960 Brown University, Providence, Rhode Island. Studied History of Art   1960-61 Ludwig Maximilian University, Munich. MA in Psychology   1964 University of Wisconsin, Madison, Wisconsin. 1962-68 Produced and directed eight films. 1970 to the present, co-founder and Editor *Radical Software*. 1971 to the present, President of Raindance, a video communication arts foundation. Lives in New York.   **Selected Individual Exhibitions**   1974 *Manhatten Is an Island* The Kitchen, New York; *From Film to Video* Anthology Film Archives, New York.   1975 The Kitchen, New York: **Selected Group Exhibitions**   1969 *Television As a Creative Medium* Howard Wise Gallery, New York.   1970 *Vision and Television* Rose Art Museum, Brandeis University, Waltham, Massachusetts.   1974 *Circuit: A Video Invitational* Everson Museum of Art, Syracuse, New York; *Art Now '74* John F. Kennedy Center for the Performing Arts, Washington, D.C.; Everson Museum of Art, Syracuse, New York; *Art/Video Confrontation 74* Musée d'Art Moderne de la Ville de Paris, Paris; *Avant-Garde Festival* New York. **Video Environments and Theater Work**   1969 Global Village, New York.   1971 Rhode Island School of Design, Providence, Rhode Island.   1972 *Matrix International Video Conference* Vancouver, British Columbia.   **Broadcasts**   1972 Cable TV, Channel D, New York. Associate Producer with Top Value Television of Democratic and Republican National Conventions, broadcast by Metromedia.

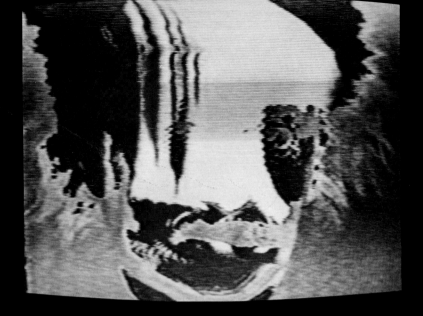

You are the product of t.v.

You are delivered to the advertiser who is the customer.

Eric Siegel Born 1944 in New York. In 1968 experimented with video feedback. Invented Processing Chrominance Synthesizer in 1968 and Electronic Video Synthesizer in 1970. During 1972-73 traveled in India, studied Hindu medicine and made videotapes. Lives in New York.

Richard Serra Born 1939 in San Francisco. BA, University of California, Berkeley; MFA, Yale University, New Haven, Connecticut. Lives in New York. **Selected Individual Exhibitions** 1966 Galleria La Salita, Rome. 1968 Galerie Ricke, Cologne. 1970 Leo Castelli Gallery, New York; Pasadena Museum of Art, Pasadena, California. 1974 The School of Visual Arts, New York. **Selected Group Exhibitions** 1968 *Annual* Whitney Museum of American Art, New York. 1969 *Square Pegs in Round Holes* Stedelijk Museum, Amsterdam; *When Attitude Becomes Form* Kunsthalle, Bern, Switzerland; *Anti-Illusion: Procedures/Materials* Whitney Museum of American Art, New York; *Theodoran Foundation: Nine Young Artists* The Solomon R. Guggenheim Museum, New York; *Art by Telephone* Museum of Contemporary Art, Chicago; *10th International Art Exhibition of Japan* Tokyo. 1970 *Annual* Whitney Museum of American Art, New York; *Sixth International Exhibition* The Solomon R. Guggenheim Museum, New York; *Prospect '71: Projection* Kunsthalle, Düsseldorf; *Art and Technology* Los Angeles County Museum of Art, Los Angeles; *Sonsbeek '71*, Arnhem, The Netherlands. 1972 *Documenta 5* Kassel, West Germany. 1973 *Options and Alternatives—Some Directions in Recent Art* Yale University Art Gallery, New Haven, Connecticut; *Contemporanea* Rome. 1974 *Line As Language: Six Artists Draw* The Art Museum, Princeton University, Princeton, New Jersey; *Art Now '74* John F. Kennedy Center for the Performing Arts, Washington, D.C.; *Project '74* Cologne.

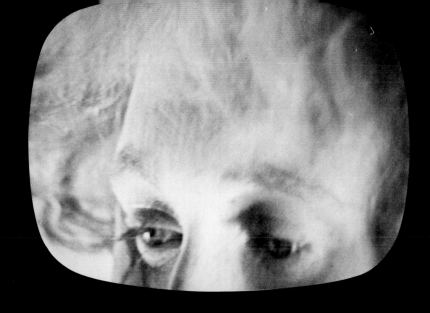

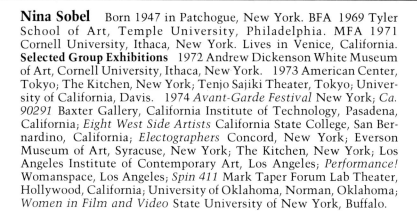

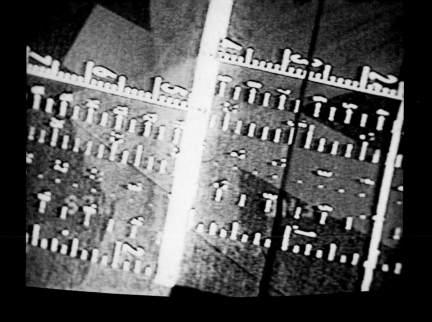

Nina Sobel Born 1947 in Patchogue, New York. BFA 1969 Tyler School of Art, Temple University, Philadelphia. MFA 1971 Cornell University, Ithaca, New York. Lives in Venice, California. **Selected Group Exhibitions** 1972 Andrew Dickenson White Museum of Art, Cornell University, Ithaca, New York. 1973 American Center, Tokyo; The Kitchen, New York; Tenjo Sajiki Theater, Tokyo; University of California, Davis. 1974 *Avant-Garde Festival* New York; *Ca. 90291* Baxter Gallery, California Institute of Technology, Pasadena, California; *Eight West Side Artists* California State College, San Bernardino, California; *Electographers* Concord, New York; Everson Museum of Art, Syracuse, New York; The Kitchen, New York; Los Angeles Institute of Contemporary Art, Los Angeles; *Performance!* Womanspace, Los Angeles; *Spin 411* Mark Taper Forum Lab Theater, Hollywood, California; University of Oklahoma, Norman, Oklahoma; *Women in Film and Video* State University of New York, Buffalo.

Keith Sonnier Born 1941 in Mamou, Louisiana. BA 1963 The University of Southwestern Louisiana, Lafayette, Louisiana. MFA 1966 Rutgers—The State University, New Brunswick, New Jersey. 1974 Guggenheim Fellowship. Lives in New York. **Selected Individual Exhibitions** 1966 Galerie Ricke, Cologne. 1970 Stedelijk van Abbemuseum, Eindhoven, The Netherlands. 1971 The Museum of Modern Art, New York. 1974 Leo Castelli Gallery, New York. **Selected Group Exhibitions** 1967 *Nine at Leo Castelli* Castelli Warehouse, New York. 1969 *When Attitude Becomes Form* Kunsthalle, Bern, Switzerland; *Square Pegs in Round Holes* Stedelijk Museum, Amsterdam; *Anti-Illusion: Procedures and Materials* Whitney Museum of American Art, New York. 1970 *69th American Exhibition* The Art Institute of Chicago, Chicago; *10th International Exhibition of Japan* Tokyo; *Information* The Museum of Modern Art, New York; *Against Order: Chance and Art* Institute of Contemporary Art, University of Pennsylvania, Philadelphia; *Annual* Whitney Museum of American Art, New York. 1971 *Prospect '71: Projection* Kunsthalle, Düsseldorf; *Biennale* Venice. 1973 *Options and Alternatives—Some Directions in Recent American Art* Yale University Art Gallery, New Haven, Connecticut; *3D Into 2D: 6 Drawings for Sculpture* The New York Cultural Center, New York; *Festival of Contemporary Art* Oberlin College, Oberlin, Ohio; *Contemporanea* Rome. 1974 *Art Now '74* John F. Kennedy Center for the Performing Arts, Washington, D.C.; *Project '74* Cologne.

Lisa Steele   Born 1947 in Kansas City, Missouri. 1965-68 University of Missouri, Kansas City, Missouri. Emigrated 1968 to Canada. Video coordinator 1972-74 A Space Gallery, Toronto. Lives in Toronto. **Selected Exhibitions** 1972 *Women and Photography* Baldwin Street Gallery of Photography, Toronto and Centaur Gallery, Montreal. 1973 *Canada Trajectoires* Musée d'Art Moderne de la Ville de Paris, Paris; *After Paris* A Space Gallery, Toronto. 1974 Everson Museum of Art, Syracuse, New York; *Videoscape* Art Gallery of Ontario, Toronto; *In Pursuit of Contemporary Art* Art Gallery of Ontario, Toronto. 1975 *A Response to the Environment* Art Gallery, Rutgers—The State University, New Brunswick, New Jersey.

Skip Sweeney   Born 1946 in Burlingame, California. BA in Theater Arts 1968 University of Santa Clara, Santa Clara, California. Founded *Electric Eye* 1969 a group for video performances and experiments. Co-founded 1970 with Arthur Ginsberg *Video Free America*. Lives in San Francisco.   **Selected Group Exhibitions** 1971 *Video Show* Whitney Museum of American Art, New York. 1973 *Video As Art* Paris. **Works** 1970 *Philo T. Farnsworth Video Obelisk* San Francisco. 1971 Video for Heathcote Williams's *AC/DC* Chelsea Theater Center, New York (with Arthur Ginsberg). 1972 Visual effects for Allen Ginsberg's *Kaddish* Chelsea Theater Center, New York (with Arthur Ginsberg). 1973 Visual effects for Peter Handke's *Kaspar* Chelsea Theater Center, New York (with Arthur Ginsberg). **Events and Performances** 1971 University Art Museum, University of California, Berkeley. 1972 Video Free America Studio, San Francisco. 1973 The Kitchen, New York; Repertory Dance Theater, University of Utah, Salt Lake City, Utah. 1974 *Avant-Garde Festival* New York.

Telethon

Billy Adler   Born 1940 in New York. BA 1962 University of Pennsylvania, Philadelphia. MA 1963 Annenberg School of Communications, University of Pennsylvania, Philadelphia. Lives in Los Angeles. **John Margolies**   Born 1940 in New York. BA 1962 University of Pennsylvania, Philadelphia. MA 1964 Annenberg School of Communications, University of Pennsylvania, Philadelphia. 1964-68 Assistant Editor, *Architectural Record*. 1966-68 Chairman, Current Work, Architectural League of New York. 1969-70 Resident Thinker, American Federation of Arts, New York. Lives in New York.   **Group History**   In 1970 Adler and Margolies formed *Telethon*, a collaboration concerned with the documentation and presentation of environmental phenomena. In 1972 *Telethon* founded The Television Collection, The Art Galleries, University of California, Santa Barbara. Published with Van Schley and Ilene Segalove "The T.V. Environment" in *Radical Software*, February 1973; "Roadside Mecca in California" in *Progressive Architecture*, June 1973.   **Selected Exhibitions**   1970 *Morris Lapidus: Architecture of Joy* Architectural League, New York; *Recorded Activities* Moore College of Art, Philadelphia.   1971 *21st International Design Conference* Aspen, Colorado; Pasadena Museum of Art, Pasadena, California; University Art Museum, University of California, Berkeley; Vancouver Art Gallery, Vancouver, British Columbia; Baltimore Museum of Art, Baltimore, Maryland.   1972 The Art Galleries, University of California, Santa Barbara; Contemporary Arts Museum, Houston, Texas.   1974 *Project '74* Cologne.

Top Value Television

TVTV   is an experimental production group formed in 1972 from the alternate television collectives, Raindance and Ant Farm, to cover the Democratic and Republican Conventions. The twelve to twenty-eight TVTV members are dedicated to the development of the portable video system as a broadcast tool for non-fiction programming. Core staff is composed of Michael Couzens, Betsy Guigon, Hudson Marquez, Allen Rucker, Michael Shamberg, Tom Weinberg and Megan Williams. Headquarters in Los Angeles.   **Selected Broadcasts**   1972 *The World's Largest Television Studio; Four More Yeares*. 1973 *The Lord of the Universe* (co-produced with WNET-TV New York); *Adland* (co-produced in collaboration with WWTW-TV Chicago).   1975 *Gerald Ford's America* (co-produced with WNET-TV New York); *The Good Times Are Killin' Me*.

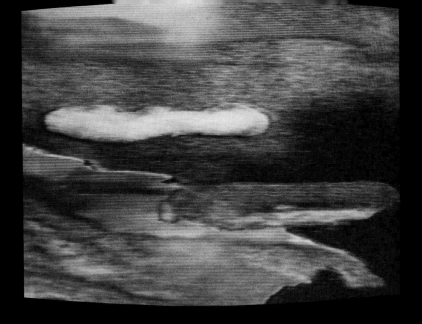

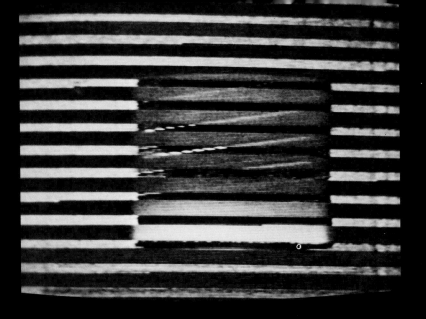

Steina and Woody Vasulka

Steina Vasulka   Born in Reykjavik, Iceland. Studied violin at Music School in Reykjavik and The Conservatory of Music in Prague. Played in Icelandic Symphony Orchestra and free-lanced in New York.
Woody Vasulka   Born in Czechoslovakia. Studied at Film Academy, Prague. Made documentary films in Algeria, Iceland, and Czechoslovakia.   1970 Woody and Steina began collaborating in experimental video.   1971 Founded The Kitchen, New York.   1972 Artists in Residence KQED-TV San Francisco.   1973 Artists in Residence WNET-TV New York. The Vasulkas live in New York.   **Selected Individual Exhibitions**   1973 *Circuit: A Video Invitational* Everson Museum of Art, Syracuse, New York.   1974 *Project '74*, Cologne; *EXPRMNTL5, Fifth International Experimental Film Competition* (video department) The Royal Film Archive of Belgium, Knokke-Heist, Belgium.   1975 *Video Art* Smithsonian Institute, Washington, D.C.

Bill Viola   Born 1951 in Flushing, New York. Installed and operated 1972-73 Synapse Cable TV System, Syracuse University, Syracuse, New York. BFA 1973 Syracuse University, Syracuse, New York. Technical Consultant 1973-74 Video Installations, Everson Museum of Art, Syracuse, New York. Technical Director 1974 to the present Art/Tapes/22, Florence. Lives in Florence.   **Selected Individual Exhibitions**   1973 Everson Museum of Art, Syracuse, New York.   1974 The Kitchen, New York; de Saisset Art Gallery and Museum, University of Santa Clara, Santa Clara, California.   **Selected Group Exhibition**   1972 *St. Jude Video Invitational* de Saisset Art Gallery and Museum, University of Santa Clara, Santa Clara, California.   1973 *Circuit: A Video Invitational* Everson Museum of Art, Syracuse, New York; *Chocorua 73* Chocorua, New Hampshire; *Avant-Garde Festival* New York.   1974 *Art Now '74* John F. Kennedy Center for the Performing Arts, Washington, D.C.; *Video/Art/Impact* Galerie Impact, Lausanne, Switzerland; *Art/Video Confrontation 74* Musée d'Art Moderne de la Ville de Paris, Paris. 1975 *Biennial* Whitney Museum of American Art, New York.

Wolf Vostell   Born 1932 near Cologne. Attended Ecole Nationale des Beaux-Arts, Paris and Kunstakademie, Düsseldorf. Co-founded 1962 Fluxus in Germany. Lives in Berlin.   **Selected Individual Exhibitions**   1960 Galerie Sala Lux, Cáceres, Spain.   1961 Galerie Soleil, Paris.   1963 Smolin Gallery, New York.   1966 Something Else Gallery, New York; Kuntsverein, Cologne.   1967 Galerie René Block, Berlin.   1968 Galerie Rolf Kuhn, Aachen, West Germany.   1970 Galerie Art Intermedia, Cologne.   1971 Galerie Baecker, Bochum, West Germany.   1972 Rheinisches Landesmuseum, Bonn.   1973 Galerie Vande Loo, Munich.   1974 Musée d'Art Moderne de la Ville de Paris, Paris.   **Selected Group Exhibitions**   1963 *Salon Comparaisons* Musée d'Art Moderne de la Ville de Paris, Paris.   1966 *The Young Generation* Akademie der Künste, Berlin.   1967 *Pictures to Be Read–Poetry to Be Seen* Museum of Contemporary Art, Chicago.   1968 *Biennale* Venice. 1969 *Superlimited Books-Boxes and Things* The Jewish Museum, New York.   1970 *Art and Politics* Kunstverein, Karlsruhe, West Germany; *Happenings & Fluxus* Kunstverein, Cologne.   1971 *Multiples: The First Decade* Philadelphia Museum of Art, Philadelphia.   1972 *Sammulung Cremer* Kunstverein, Heidelberg.   1973 *Artists Books* Moore College of Art, Philadelphia; *Contemporanea* Rome.   1974 *ADA₂– Action of the Avant Garde* Neuer Berliner Kunstverein, Berlin; *Project '74* Cologne.

Morihiro Wada   Born 1947 in Takamatsu, Japan. Graduated 1973 Tama University of Art, Tokyo. Lives in Yokohama.   **Selected Individual Exhibitions**   1971 Tamura Gallery, Tokyo.   1972 Tamura Gallery, Tokyo.   1973 Tamura Gallery, Tokyo.   1974 Tamura Gallery, Tokyo; Tokiwa Gallery, Tokyo.   **Selected Group Exhibitions**   1968 *1st Shikoku Modern Art Exhibition* Takamatsu Municipal Museum, Takamatsu; *1st S.E.A. Group Exhibition* Gallery Miyatake, Takamatsu.   1970 *Kyoto Field Creation Exhibition* Kamo River, Kyoto; *2nd Ehime Field Art Festival* Matsuyama.   1971 *6th Japan Art Festival* The National Museum of Modern Art, Tokyo; *6th International Young Artists Exhibition* Takanawa Art Museum, Tokyo; *Operation* Tama University of Art, Tokyo.   1972 *Do-It-Yourself-Kit/ Video Communication* Sony Building, Tokyo; *7th Japan Art Festival* Tokyo Central Museum, Tokyo; *Operation Vesuvio* Minami Gallery, Tokyo; *Fine Arts Manifesto Exhibition* Tokyo.   1973 *What Did Suzuki Do at Tama River* Tama River, Tokyo; *Inter-Subjective Existance Construction* Tamura Gallery, Tokyo; *Tokyo–New York Video Express* Tenjo-Sajiki-Kan, Tokyo; *1st Film Media* Tamura Gallery, Tokyo.   1974 *Tokyo Biennial* Tokyo Metropolitan Art Museum, Tokyo; *Image Today* Tokyo.

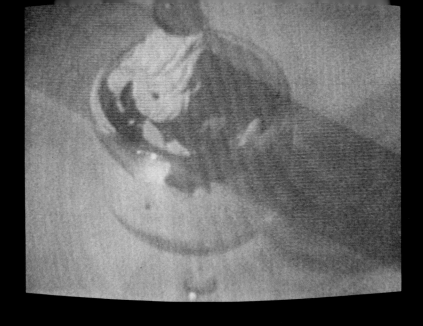

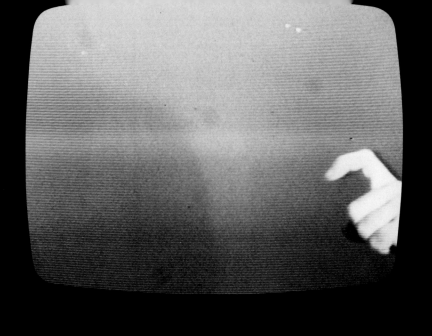

Andy Warhol   Born 1930 in Philadelphia. Studied Carnegie Institute of Technology, Pittsburgh, and Philadelphia College of Art, Philadelphia. Lives in New York. **Selected Individual Exhibitions** 1962 Ferus Gallery, Los Angeles. 1964 Stable Gallery, New York. 1965 Institute of Contemporary Art, University of Pennsylvania, Philadelphia. 1966 Leo Castelli, New York. 1968 Moderna Museet, Stockholm. 1970 Museum of Contemporary Art, Chicago; Stedelijk van Abbemuseum, Eindhoven, The Netherlands. 1971 Tate Gallery, London; Whitney Museum of American Art, New York. 1972 Walker Art Center, Minneapolis. **Selected Group Exhibitions** 1962 *New Realists* Sidney Janis Gallery, New York. 1963 *The Popular Image* Institute of Contemporary Arts, London. 1964 *Amerikanst Pop Konst* Moderna Museet, Stockholm; *The Atmosphere of '64* Institute of Contemporary Art, University of Pennsylvania, Philadelphia. 1965 *Pop Art Nouveau Réalism Etc...* Palais des Beaux-Arts, Brussels. 1967 *Bienal São Paulo.* 1968 *Documenta 4* Kassel, West Germany. 1969 *Painting in New York 1944-1969* Pasadena Art Museum, Pasedena, California. 1971 *Prospect '71: Projection* Kunsthalle, Düsseldorf. 1974 *Contemporanea,* Rome; *American Pop Art* Whitney Museum of American Art, New York. **Selected Film Activities** 1963-64 *Eat; Sleep* and other "motionless," black and white movies. 1965 *My Hustler.* 1966 *Chelsea Girls.* 1968 *Lonesome Cowboys; Blue Movie.*

William Wegman   Born 1943 in Holyoke, Massachusetts. BFA 1965 Massachusetts College of Art, Boston; MFA 1967 University of Illinois, Urbana, Illinois. Lives in New York. **Selected Individual Exhibitions** 1971 Pomona College Art Gallery, Pomona, California; Galerie Ileana Sonnabend, Paris. 1972 Galerie Konrad Fischer, Düsseldorf; Galerie Ernst, Hanover, West Germany. 1974 Gallery D, Brussels; Galleria Toselli, Milan. **Selected Group Exhibitions** 1968 *1968 Biennial of Painting and Sculpture* Walker Art Center, Minneapolis, Minnesota; *Media 1968* Kohler Art Center, Sheboygan, Wisconsin; Milwaukee Art Center, Milwaukee, Wisconsin. 1969 *Plan and Project in Art* Kunsthalle, Bern, Switzerland; *Soft Art I* New Jersey State Museum, Trenton, New Jersey; *When Attitude Becomes Form* Kunsthalle, Bern, Switzerland; *Other Ideas* The Detroit Institute of Art, Detroit, Michigan; *Art by Telephone* Museum of Contemporary Art, Chicago; *Place and Process* Edmonton Art Gallery, Edmonton, Alberta. 1970 *Art in the Mind* Allen Memorial Museum, Oberlin College, Oberlin, Ohio; *Body Images* Museum of Conceptual Art, San Francisco. 1971 *24 Young Los Angeles Artists* Los Angeles County Museum of Art, Los Angeles; *Pier 18* The Museum of Modern Art, New York; *Prospect '71: Projection* Kunsthalle, Düsseldorf; *11 Los Angeles Artists* Hayward Gallery, London. 1972 *Documenta 5* Kassel, West Germany. 1973 *Circuit: A Video Invitational* Everson Museum of Art, Syracuse, New York; *Annual* Whitney Museum of American Art, New York. 1974 *Project '74* Cologne.

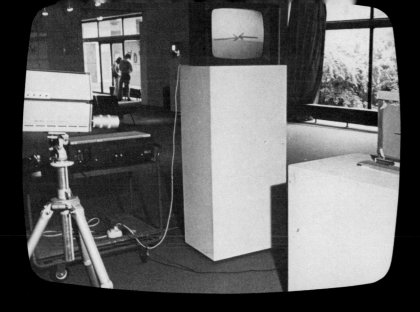

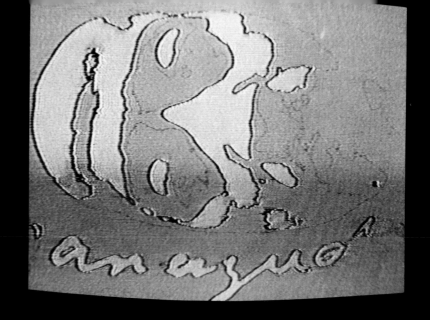

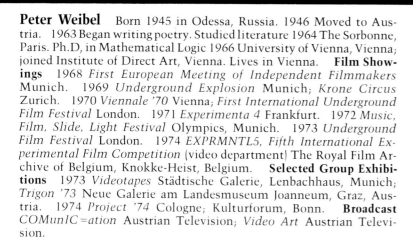

Peter Weibel Born 1945 in Odessa, Russia. 1946 Moved to Austria. 1963 Began writing poetry. Studied literature 1964 The Sorbonne, Paris. Ph.D, in Mathematical Logic 1966 University of Vienna, Vienna; joined Institute of Direct Art, Vienna. Lives in Vienna. **Film Showings** 1968 *First European Meeting of Independent Filmmakers* Munich. 1969 *Underground Explosion* Munich; *Krone Circus* Zurich. 1970 *Viennale '70* Vienna; *First International Underground Film Festival* London. 1971 *Experimenta 4* Frankfurt. 1972 *Music, Film, Slide, Light Festival* Olympics, Munich. 1973 *Underground Film Festival* London. 1974 *EXPRMNTL5, Fifth International Experimental Film Competition* (video department) The Royal Film Archive of Belgium, Knokke-Heist, Belgium. **Selected Group Exhibitions** 1973 *Videotapes* Städtische Galerie, Lenbachhaus, Munich; *Trigon '73* Neue Galerie am Landesmuseum Joanneum, Graz, Austria. 1974 *Project '74* Cologne; Kulturforum, Bonn. **Broadcast** *COMunIC=ation* Austrian Television; *Video Art* Austrian Television.

Katsuhiro Yamaguchi Born 1928 in Tokyo. Graduated 1951 Law Department of Japan University, Tokyo. 1951 Joined Jikken Kobo Experimental Studio and began work as a sculptor and experimental designer. 1968 Published *Amorphous Esthetics*. 1970 Chief designer for the Mitsui Pavilion, *Expo '70* Osaka. 1971 Began work in video. Lives in Tokyo. **Selected Exhibitions** 1955 *The 1st Exhibition of Contemporary Japanese Sculpture* Ube Museum, Ube. 1965 *New Japanese Painting and Sculpture* San Francisco Museum of Art, San Francisco and The Museum of Modern Art, New York. 1967 *The 5th International Guggenheim Exhibition* The Solomon R. Guggenheim Museum, New York. 1968 *The 8th Exhibition of Contemporary Japanese Art* National Museum of Art, Tokyo. 1968 *Contemporary Sculpture* Suma Rikyu Koen, Kobe; *Biennale* Venice. 1969 *Arts '69* Helsinki; *Electromagica* Tokyo. *World Contemporary Art–Dialogue Between the East and the West* National Museum of Art, Tokyo; *1st International Exhibition of Modern Sculpture* Hakone Museum, Hakone.

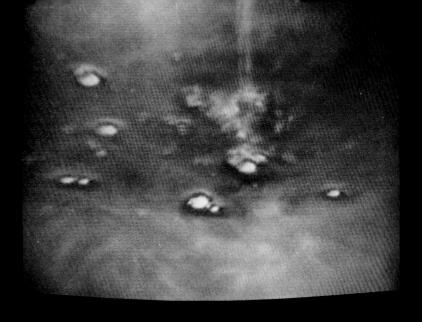

Keigo Yamamoto   Born 1936 in Fukui, Japan. Graduated 1958 Fukui University, Fukui. Lives in Fukui City.   **Selected Individual Exhibitions**   1966 Mudo Gallery, Tokyo.   1967 Ano Gallery, Osaka; Beni Gallery, Kyoto.   1968 Muramatsu Gallery, Tokyo.   1969 *Fire Event Series* Fukui (first exhibition of videotape).   1970 *The Earth— From Myth Effect* Muramatsu Gallery, Tokyo.   1972 *From a Series of Confirmation by Action* Gallery 16, Tokyo.   **Selected Group Exhibitions**   1968 *8th Contemporary Art Exhibition of Japan* Tokyo Metropolitan Art Museum, Tokyo.   1969 *The Nine Light Exhibit* Iteza Gallery, Kyoto.   1972 *Operation Vesuvio* Minami Gallery, Tokyo; *Video Week* American Center, Tokyo; *Equivalent Cinema '72* Municipal Museum of Fine Arts, Kyoto.   1973 *The Matrix International Video Conference* Vancouver Art Gallery, Vancouver, British Columbia; *Kyoto Biennial '73* Municipal Museum of Fine Arts, Kyoto; *International Film Festival* Pessaro, Italy.   1974 *Tokyo–New York Video Express* Tenjo-Sajiki-Kan, Tokyo; *The '73-'74 Contemporary Art* Art Core Hall, Kyoto; *Tokyo Biennial '74* Tokyo Metropolitan Art Museum, Tokyo; *Video Communication* Art Core Hall, Kyoto; *New Music Media Festival* Karuizawa; *The Video Game Festival* Karuizawa; *The Japan Art Festival* Musée d'Art Contemporain, Montreal; *Nature Deprived* Fukui Housou Kaikan, Fukui; *Video-Kyoto 1974* Gallery Signum, Kyoto.

Commercials   Twenty-two broadcast commercials from Germany, Japan, Spain, Sweden and the United States from 1948 to 1973. Selected by Institute of Contemporary Art, Philadelphia with the aid of Michael Demetriades, Clio, New York.

CATALOGUE TO THE EXHIBITION

CATALOGUE TO THE EXHIBITION

Installation Works

Dimensions are given in feet; height precedes length precedes width. The measurements below will change somewhat at each institution.

Peter Campus

col 1974
a video camera with a tivicon tube, tripod, rear screen projector, red light
10 x 32 x 15
courtesy of Bykert Gallery, New York

Douglas Davis

Images from the Present Tense I 1971
a 1962 black and white TV
16 x 22 x 12
lent by Finch College Museum of Art, New York

Dan Graham

Present Continuous Pasts 1974
a black and white video camera and monitor, two reel to reel tape players, a half-inch video loop, four sheets of plastic mirror, each four by eight feet, fluorescent lights, spun glass cloth
8 x 8 x 8
the artist

Paul Kos

REVOLUTION: Notes for the Invasion MAR MAR MARCH 1972-1973
redwood two-by-fours, a red box with typewriter, manuscript and one-inch TV, cassette player and videotape:
MAR MAR MARCH 1972-1973, black and white, 12 minutes, sound, camerawork by Marlene Kos, produced at University of Santa Clara Studio, Santa Clara, California
10 x 21 x 15
the artist

Les Levine

Contact: A Cybernetic Sculpture 1969
eighteen black and white TVs, nine cameras
9 x 9 x 6
lent by The New York Cultural Center in association with Fairleigh Dickinson University, New York

Nam June Paik

TV Garden 1974
fifteen color TVs, five black and white TVs, four electric fans, cassette player, splitters, amplifier, plants, videotape:
Global Grove 1973, color, 30 minutes, sound, produced at WNET-TV Lab, New York
10 x 20 x 15
courtesy of Bonino Gallery, New York

Videotapes

Length of tapes is given in minutes and seconds.

Vito Acconci

Undertone 1972 black and white 30 sound
distributed by Castelli-Sonnabend Tapes and Films, Inc., New York

Sonia Andrade

Untitled 1974 black and white 10 sound
technical assistance: Jom Azulay
lent by Museu de Arte Contemporânea da Universidade de São Paulo, São Paulo

Ant Farm

The Cadillac Ranch Show 1974 color 30 sound
camerawork: Antfarm, KVII-TV
produced at KVII-TV, Amarillo, Texas
distributed by Electronic Arts Intermix, Inc., New York

Eleanor Antin

The Ballerina and the Bum 1974 black and white 52 sound
distributed by The Video Distribution, Inc., New York

David Askevold

My Recall of an Imprint from a Hypothetical Jungle 1973 black and white 6 sound
It's No Use Crying 1971 black and white 3 sound
Concert Cover 1972 black and white 6 sound
distributed by Art Metropole, Toronto

John Baldessari
Inventory 1972 black and white 30 sound
distributed by Castelli-Sonnabend Tapes and
Films, Inc., New York

Lynda Benglis
Collage 1973 color 9.35 sound
distributed by Castelli-Sonnabend Tapes and
Films, Inc., New York

Jim Byrne
Both 1974 black and white 5 sound
camerawork: Tim Harding
Translucent 1974 black and white 5 sound
Hand Held #2 1974 black and white 5 sound
the artist

Pierpaolo Calzolari
No Title 1974 black and white 8 sound
technical assistance: Raffaele Corazziari,
Alberto Pirelli
produced at Art/Tapes/22
distributed by Art/Tapes/22, Florence

Colin Campbell
Sackville, I'm Yours 1972 black and white
15 sound
distributed by Art Metropole, Toronto

Peter Campus
Set of Co-Incidence 1974 color 15 sound
produced at WGBH-TV Workshop, Boston, with
support from National Endowment for the Arts
and The Rockefeller Foundation
distributed by Castelli-Sonnabend Tapes and
Films, Inc., New York

Giuseppe Chiari
The Sound 1974 black and white 18 sound
technical assistance: Andrea Giorgi
produced at Art/Tapes/22
distributed by Art/Tapes/22, Florence

Fernando França Cocchiarale
You Are Time 1974 black and white 10 sound
technical assistance: Jom Azulay
Memory 1974 black and white 10 sound
technical assistance: Jom Azulay
lent by Museu de Arte Contemporânea da
Universidade de São Paulo, São Paulo

Andrea Daninos
Show of Everybody's Death 1974 black and white
8 sound
technical assistance: Raffaele Corazziari,
Alberto Pirelli
produced at Art/Tapes/22
distributed by Art/Tapes/22, Florence

Antonio Dias
*Illustration of Art on the Use of Multimedia
(Rat Music and Banana for Two)* 1974 black and
white 14 sound
produced at Art/Tapes/22
distributed by Art/Tapes/22, Florence

Juan Downey
Chile 1974 color 15 sound
distributed by The Video Distribution, Inc.,
New York
Video Dances 1974 black and white 30 sound
dancers: Carmen Beuchat, Barbara Dilley
produced at Electronic Arts Intermix, Inc.
distributed by Electronic Arts Intermix, Inc.,
New York

Ed Emshwiller
Scape-Mates 1972 color 29 sound
dancers: Emery Hermans, Sarah Sheldon
technical assistance: Walter Wright, Richard
Froman, John Godfrey
produced at Dolphin and WNET-TV Lab,
New York
distributed by Electronic Arts Intermix, Inc.,
New York

Valie Export
Space Seeing and–Hearing I, II, III, IV, V 1974
black and white 20 sound
camerawork: Lijnbaancentrum Rotterdamse
Kunstichting
music: Christian Michelin, Valie Export
produced at Kunstverein, Cologne
the artist

Terry Fox
Children's Tapes 1974 black and white
28.30 sound
the artist

Howard Fried
seaquick 1972-1975 black and white 34 sound
camerawork: George Bolling, Tyrus Gerlach
sound: Bruce Bangsberg
produced at the University of Santa Clara, Santa
Clara, California and San Francisco Art Institute
the artist

Seiichi Fujii
Mantra 1973 black and white 7 sound
produced at Video Hiroba
distributed by Video Hiroba, Tokyo

Anna Bella Geiger
Centerminal 1974 black and white 7 sound
technical assistance: Jom Azulay
Passages 1974 black and white 3 sound
technical assistance: Jom Azulay
Statement in Portrait 1974 black and white
20 sound
technical assistance: Jom Azulay
lent by Museu de Arte Contemporânea da
Universidade de São Paulo, São Paulo

Michael Geissler & VAM
Ich will nicht nach Casablanca 1974 black and
white 20 sound
distributed by Video Audio Medien, Berlin

General Idea
Light on Double Mirror Video 1971-1974 black and white 26 sound
distributed by Art Metropole, Toronto

Frank Gillette
Tetragramaton 1973 black and white 26 sound
distributed by Castelli-Sonnabend Tapes and Films, Inc., New York

Sakumi Hagiwara
Reprint 1973 black and white 5 sound
produced at Video Hiroba
Twenty Years 1974 black and white 5.35 sound
produced at Video Hiroba
distributed by Video Hiroba, Tokyo

Martha Haslanger
Outlines 1973 black and white 8.10 silent
the artist

Michael Hayden
Scan/Gaspe 1973 black and white 15 sound
produced at Sony Video Studios, Toronto
the artist

K. H. Hödicke
Tartaruga 1968 color 3 sound
ADI (for Duchamp) 1971 color
3 sound
ADII, In Advance of the Broken Leg 1971 color
3 sound
La Faccia del Mondo 1971 color 3 sound
Tivoli 1971 color 3 sound
Zähne 1971 color 3 sound
distributed by Galerie René Block, Berlin

Nancy Holt
Underscan 1974 black and white 8 sound
technical assistance: Carlota Schoolman
distributed by Castelli-Sonnabend Tapes and Films, Inc., New York

Rebecca Horn
Masken 1973 black and white 18 sound
camerawork: Helmut Weitz
produced at The Film Academy, Berlin
the artist

Mako Idemitsu
What a Woman Made 1974 black and white 13.35 sound
produced at Video Hiroba
distributed by Video Hiroba, Tokyo

Taka Iimura
I Love You 1974 black and white 7 sound
distributed by The Videotape Distribution, Inc., New York

Joan Jonas
Vertical Roll 1972 black and white 20 sound
Disturbances 1974 black and white 14 sound
distributed by Castelli-Sonnabend Tapes and Films, Inc., New York

Allan Kaprow
The 2nd Routine 1974 black and white 15 sound
produced by The Video Distribution, Inc.
distributed by The Video Distribution, Inc., New York

Nobuhiro Kawanaka
Playback No. 7 1974 black and white 11 sound
produced at Video Hiroba
distributed by Video Hiroba, Tokyo

Hakudo Kobayashi
Earth 1974 color 10.20 sound
produced at Toyo-Genzo-Sho, Tokyo
distributed by Video Hiroba, Tokyo

Masao Komura
Object Collection '74 1974 color 7.40 sound
distributed by Video Hiroba, Tokyo

Beryl Korot and Ira Schneider
4th of July in Saugerties 1972 black and white 20 sound
produced at Raindance, New York
distributed by Electronic Arts Intermix, Inc., New York

Ernie Kovacs
Kovacs! 1951-1961 black and white 60 sound
distributed by Video Tape Network, Inc., New York

Shigeko Kubota
Europe on ½ Inch a Day 1971 black and white 30 sound
distributed by Electronic Arts Intermix, Inc., New York

Richard Landry
Divided Alto 1974 color 15 sound
distributed by Castelli-Sonnabend Tapes and Films, Inc., New York

Alvin Lucier
The Queen of the South 1974 black and white 30 sound
this tape is an outgrowth of a live performance commissioned in 1972 by Gerald Shapiro, The New Music Ensemble, Providence, Rhode Island
produced at Art/Tapes/22
distributed by Art/Tapes/22, Florence

Urs Lüthi
Morir d'Amore 1974 black and white 9 sound
technical assistance: Andrea Giorgi, Germano Sangirardi, Enzo Stella
performers: Urs and Elke Lüthi
Untitled 1974 black and white 11 sound
technical assistance: Andrea Giorgi, Lesley Pinnock, Enzo Stella, Germano Sangirardi
produced at Art/Tapes/22 in collaboration with Galleria Diagramma, Milan
distributed by Art/Tapes/22, Florence

Ivens Olinto Machado
Slave Maker Slave 1974 black and white 10 sound
technical assistance: Jom Azulay
Dissolution 1974 black and white 10 sound
technical assistance: Jom Azulay
Versus 1974 black and white 10 sound
technical assistance: Jom Azulay
lent by Museu de Arte Contemporânea da
Universidade de Sâo Paulo, Sâo Paulo

Andy Mann
Hie Noon 1973 black and white 10.30 sound
distributed by Electronic Arts Intermix, Inc.,
New York

Toshio Matsumoto
Expansion 1972 color 14 sound
audio assistance: Toshi Ichiyanagi
distributed by Video Hiroba, Tokyo

Kyoko Michishita
"Let's Have a Dream"—Yoko Ono in Japan 1974
black and white 11.30 sound
produced at Video Hiroba
distributed by Video Hiroba, Tokyo

Robert Morris
Exchange 1973 black and white 32 sound
distributed by Castelli-Sonnabend Tapes and
Films, Inc., New York

Philip Morton
Colorfull Colorada...Tuesday on the Way to Work
1974 color 20 sound
utilizes the Sandin Image Processor, an analog
computer
the artist

Fujiko Nakaya
Statics of an Egg 1973 black and white 11 sound
produced at Video Hiroba
distributed by Video Hiroba, Tokyo

Bruce Nauman
Lip Sync 1969 black and white 60 sound
distributed by Castelli-Sonnabend Tapes and
Films, Inc., New York

Dennis Oppenheim
*2-Stage Transfer Drawing (Returning to a Past
State)* 1971 black and white 8 sound
performers: Erik and Dennis Oppenheim
*2-Stage Transfer Drawing (Advancing to a Future
State)* 1971 black and white 13 sound
performers: Dennis and Erik Oppenheim
distributed by The Video Distribution, Inc.,
New York

Jean Otth
Limite E 1973 black and white 10 sound
technical assistance: Serge Menendoz
produced at Galerie Impact, Lausanne
Limite B (Le Lac) 1973 black and white 12 sound
technical assistance: Serge Menendoz
produced at Galerie Impact, Lausanne
distributed by Art/Tapes/22, Florence

Giulio Paolini
Unisono 1974 black and white 2 silent
produced at Art/Tapes/22
distributed by Art/Tapes/22, Florence

Ulrike Rosenbach
Der Mann sei das Haupt der Frau 1972 black and
white 8 sound
Videoconcert 2, Inselmusik 1974 black and white
10 sound
distributed by Galerie Ingrid Oppenheim, Cologne

Reiner Ruthenbeck
*Object zur teilweisen Verdeckung einer
Videoszene* 1972 black and white 30 sound
camerawork: Lijnbaancentrum Rotterdamse
Kunstichting
the artist

Daniel Sandin
*Amplitude Classified Clouds, Romp and Roust
through the Image Processor* 1974 color 16 sound
utilizes the Sandin Image Processor, an analog
computer
the artist

Ira Schneider
Bits, Chunks & Pieces 1975 black and white
45 sound
produced at Raindance and Electronic Arts
Intermix, Inc., New York
the artist

Eric Siegel
*Einstine, Symphony of the Planets, Tomorrow
Never Knows* 1968 colorized black and white
20 sound
distributed by Electronic Arts Intermix, Inc.,
New York

Richard Serra
Television Delivers People 1973 color 6 sound
technical assistance: Carlota Schoolman
distributed by Castelli-Sonnabend Tapes and
Films, Inc., New York

Nina Sobel
Breakdowns 1974 black and white 23.30 sound
camerawork: John Sturgeon
distributed by Newspace Gallery, Los Angeles

Keith Sonnier
Mat Key Radio Track 1972 color 10 sound
performers: Tina Girouard, Suzanne Harris
Animation II 1974 color 25 sound
produced at Computer Image, Denver, Colorado
distributed by Castelli-Sonnabend Tapes and
Films, Inc., New York

Lisa Steele
Lisa and the Egg 1972 black and white 18 sound
camerawork: Tom Sherman
A Very Personal Story 1974 black and white
20 sound
distributed by Art Metropole, Toronto

Skip Sweeney

Moogvidium 1972 colorized black and white
15.55 sound
camerawork: Arthur Ginsberg
Moog synthesizer: Douglas McKechine
vidium: Bill Hearn
produced at Video Free America, San Francisco
the artist

Telethon

Television Highlights 1972-1974 color 30 sound
with segments from *Our National Anthem,
Pillsbury Bakeoff, Bowling for Dollars* with Chick
Hearn, *Let's Make a Deal* with Monty Hall, *Brady
Bunch, Partridge Family, All in the Family, An
American Family, Mark Spitz, Howdy Doody,
George Jessel, Spiro Agnew, Dr. Pepper, Double-
mint Twins, Texaco, MacDonalds, Andy Williams
Christmas Special, Miss America 1973, Mr. World
1973, Belmont Stakes 1973, Munich Olympics
1972, Inauguration 1972 AMERICA, John W. Dean
III, Richard Nixon Resigns, Jerry Lewis*

Television History 1974 black and white 60 sound
with segments from *Rin Tin Tin* ca. 1954, *Nabisco
Honeys Commercial* ca. 1954, *You Asked for It*
with Art Baker 1955, *Howdy Doody* with Bob
Smith 1958, *Wonder Bread Commercial* 1958,
Gene Autry 1950, *Highway Patrol* 1957, *Sea Hunt*
1960, *Ozzie and Harriet* 1956, *I Love Lucy* 1953,
Sergeant Bilko with Phil Silvers 1959, *Queen for a
Day* starring Jack Baily 1959, *Timex Commercial*
with John Cameron Swayze 1956, *Liberace* 1954,
Muriel Cigar Commercial with Edie Adams 1953,
Chance of a Lifetime starring Dennis James 1953,
Old Gold Cigarette Commercial from *Chance of a
Lifetime* starring Dennis James 1953, *See It Now*
with Edward R. Murrow, McCarthy sequence
1953, *Perry Mason* 1955, *Alfred Hitchcock* 1954,
The Continental 1953, *Steve Allen Show* with
Elvis Presley 1956, *Viceroy Cigarette Commercial*
1956, *Untouchables* 1959, *Fugitive* 1966, *Lloyd
Thaxton Show* 1965, *Shebang* starring Casey Cas-
sen 1966, *Shivaree* starring Gene Weeden 1967,
Okay Mother with Dennis James 1947, *Chance of
a Lifetime* with Dennis James 1953, *What's My
Line!* with John Daly 1953, *The Price Is Right*
with Bill Cullen 1956, *Twenty-One* with Jack
Barry 1957, *Dollar a Second* with Jan Murray 1954,
Lone Ranger 1952, *Pinky Lee Show* 1956, *The
Lucy-Desi Comedy Hour* ca. 1955, *Amos 'n Andy*
1955, *Father Knows Best* 1961, *Ozzie and Harriet*
with Rick Nelson 1960
distributed by Telethon, Los Angeles

Top Value Television (TVTV)

The Lord of the Universe 1974 color 60 sound
produced in conjunction with WNET-TV,
New York
distributed by Electronic Arts Intermix, Inc.,
New York

Steina and Woody Vasulka

Golden Voyage 1973 color 27 sound
produced at Synapse Cable TV, Syracuse
University, Syracuse, New York
distributed by Electronic Arts Intermix, Inc.,
New York

Bill Viola

Information 1973 color 30 sound
produced at Synapse Cable TV, Syracuse
University, Syracuse, New York
distributed by Electronic Arts Intermix, Inc.,
New York

Wolf Vostell

Desastres 1972 color 45 sound
camerawork: Helmut Wietz
produced at Neuer Berliner Kunstverein-Videothek
distributed by Neuer Berliner Kunstverein-
Videothek, Berlin

Morihiro Wada

Situation 1974 black and white 9.30 sound
distributed by Video Hiroba, Tokyo

Andy Warhol

The Underground Sundae 1968 color 1 sound
a commercial commissioned by Schrafft's
lent by Clio, New York

William Wegman

Selected Works, Reel 2 1972 black and white
14 sound
Selected Works, Reel 3 1972 black and white
17 sound
distributed by Castelli-Sonnabend Tapes and
Films, Inc., New York

Peter Weibel

VT and TV: Selected Works 1969-1973 black and
white 20 sound
camerawork: Peter Weibel, Helmuth Fibich
the artist

Katsuhiro Yamaguchi

Video-Portrait 1973 color 7 sound
produced at Toyo-Genzo-Sho, Tokyo
distributed by Video Hiroba, Tokyo

Keigo Yamamoto

Water 1972 black and white 9.30 sound
distributed by Video Hiroba, Tokyo

Commercials

1948-1973 black and white and color 30 sound
Texaco Sky Chief with Milton Berle 1948, *Lipton
Chicken Noodle Soup* with Arthur Godfrey 1954,
S.O.S. Magic Scouring Pads 1955, *Chevrolet* 1962,
Ipana Toothpaste 1962, *Muriel Cigars* with Edie
Adams 1962, *New York Times* 1963, *Purolator Oil
Filter* 1963, *Sunsweet Marches On!* 1968, *CBS
World Watchers* 1968, *Volkswagen* 1968, *Jeno's
Pizza Rolls* 1968, *Tonik* (Sweden) ca. 1961, *Great
American Soup* ca. 1968, *Alka-Seltzer* 1972, *Na-
tional Council for Drug Abuse* 1972, *Help Unsell
the War* 1972, *ABC Wide World of Sports* 1972,
Trygg-Hansa (Sweden) 1972, *AEG Dreyer* (Ger-
many) 1972, *National Hi Top* (Japan) 1973, *Ebro
Siato* (Spain) 1973
selected by the Institute
with the aid of Michael Demetriades
lent by Clio, New York

ESSAYS

VIDEO:
THE DISTINCTIVE
FEATURES
OF THE MEDIUM
David Antin

VIDEO ART. The name is equivocal. A good name. It leaves open all the questions and asks them anyway. Is this an art form, a new genre? An anthology of valued activity conducted in a particular arena defined by display on a cathode ray tube? The kind of video made by a special class of people—artists—whose works are exhibited primarily in what is called "the art world"—ARTISTS' VIDEO? An inspection of the names in the catalogue gives the easy and not quite sufficient answer that it is this last we are considering, ARTISTS' VIDEO. But is this a class apart? Artists have been making video pieces for scarcely ten years—if we disregard one or two flimsy studio jobs and Nam June Paik's 1963 kamikaze TV modifications—and video has been a fact of gallery life for barely five years. Yet we've already had group exhibitions, panels, symposia, magazine issues devoted to this phenomenon, for the very good reason that more and more artists are using video and some of the best work being done in the art world is being done with video. Which is why a discourse has already arisen to greet it. Actually two discourses: one, a kind of enthusiastic welcoming prose peppered with fragments of communication theory and McLuhanesque media talk; the other, a rather nervous attempt to locate the "unique properties of the medium." Discourse 1 could be called "cyberscat" and Discourse 2, because it engages the issues that pass for "formalism" in the art world, could be called "the formalist rap." Though there is no necessary relation between them, the two discourses occasionally occur together as they do in the talk of Frank Gillette, which offers a convenient sample:

D₁ The emergence of relationships between the culture you're in and the parameters that allow you expression are fed back through a technology. It's the state of the art technology within a particular culture that gives shape to ideas.

D2   What I'm consciously involved in is devising a way that is structurally intrinsic to television. For example, what makes it *not* film? Part of it is that you look *into* the source of light, with film you look *with* the source of light. In television, the source of light and the source of information are one.[1]

Though it is not entirely clear what "high class" technology has to do with the rather pleasantly shabby technical state of contemporary video art, or what the significance is to human beings of the light source in two adjacent representational media, statements of this type are characteristic, and similar quotes could be multiplied endlessly. And if these concerns seem somewhat gratuitous or insufficient with respect to the work at hand, they often share a kind of aptness of detail, even though it is rarely clear what the detail explains of the larger pattern of activity in which these artists are involved. In fact what seems most typical of both types of discourse is a certain anxiety, that may be seen most clearly in a recent piece by Hollis Frampton:

> Moreover it is doubly important that we try to say what video is at present because we posit for it a privileged future. Since the birth of video art from the Jovian backside (I dare not say brow) of the Other Thing called television, I for one have felt a more and more pressing need for precise definitions of what film art *is,* since I extend to film, as well, the hope of a privileged future.[2]

It would be so much more convenient to develop the refined discussion of the possible differences between film and video, if we could only forget the Other Thing—television. Yet television haunts this exhibition, as it must haunt any exhibition of video

art. It is present here only in a few commercials and the "golden performances" of Ernie Kovacs (a television "artist"). Other television "artists" and "art works" are absent—Walter Cronkite, Sam Ervin, Ron Ziegler, the *Sid Caeser Show,* Cal Worthington, McCann-Erickson. Television is here mainly in quotes, allusion, parody and protest, as in Telethon's *TV History,* Douglas Davis's installation piece with the TV set forced to face the wall, Richard Serra's *Television Delivers People.* No doubt, in time there will be an *auteur* theory of television, which will do for Milton Berle and Sid Caeser what Sarris and Farber and *Cahiers du Cinéma* have done for John Huston and Nicholas Ray and Howard Hawks. But the politics of the art world is, for good reasons, rather hostile to Pop, and that kind of admiring discussion will have to wait; even *Cahiers du Cinéma* has abandoned Hitchcock and Nicholas Ray for Dziga Vertov and the European avant garde, on sociopolitical, aesthetic grounds. But it's unwise to despise an enemy, especially a more powerful, older enemy, who happens also to be your frightful parent. So, it is with television we have to begin to consider video, because if anything has defined the formal and technical properties of the video medium it is the television industry.

The history of television in the United States is well known. Commercial television is essentially a post second World War phenomenon, and its use was, logically enough, patterned on commercial radio, since control of the new medium was in the hands of the powerful radio networks, which constitute essentially a government protected, private monopoly. This situation determined many of the fundamental communication characteristics of the new medium.

The most basic of these is the social relation between "sending" and "receiving," which is profoundly unequal and asymmetrical. Since the main potential broadcasters, the powerful radio networks, were already deeply involved with the electronics industry through complex ownership affiliation, and since they also constituted the single largest potential customer for the electronic components of television, the components were developed entirely for their convenience and profit. While this may not seem surprising, the result was that the acts of "picture taking" and "transmission" were made enormously expensive: cameras and transmission systems were designed and priced out of the reach of anything but corporate ownership. Moreover government regulation set standards on "picture quality" and the transmission signal, which effectively ensured that "taking" and "transmission" control would remain in the hands of the industry into which the federal government had already assigned the airwaves channel by channel. The receivers alone were priced within the range of individual ownership. This fundamental ordering, establishing the relations between the taker-sender and the receiver had, of course, been worked out for commercial radio.

Only ham transmission—also hemmed in severely by government regulation—and special uses like ship-to-shore, pilot-to-control tower and police band radio deal in the otherwise merely potential equalities of wireless telephony. That this was not technically inevitable, but merely an outcome of the social situation and the marketing strategies of the industry is obvious. There is nothing necessarily more complex or expensive in the camera than there is in the receiver. It is merely that the great expense of receiver technology was defrayed by the mass production of the sets, whose multiplication multiplied the dollar exchange value of transmission time sold by the transmitter to his advertisers. So the broadcasters underwrote receiver development, because every set bought delivers its viewers as salable goods in an exchange that pays for the "expensive" technology.

For television also there is a special use domain— educational, industrial and now artistic—where the relation between the camera and receiver may be more or less equalized, but this is because transmission is not an issue and the distribution of the images is severely restricted. The economic fact remains: transmission is more expensive than reception. This ensures a power hierarchy: transmission dominates reception. And it follows from this asymmetry of power relations that the taker-transmitter dominates whatever communication takes place.

This is clearer when you consider the manners of telephony. A would-be transmitter asks for permission to transmit, rings the home of a potential receiver. It's like ringing a doorbell. Or a would-be receiver rings the home of a possible transmitter, asks him/her to transmit. This formal set of relations has become even more refined with the introduction of the *Answerphone* and the answering service, which mediates between the ring—an anonymous invitation to communicate—and the response, requiring the caller to identify himself and leaves the receiver with a choice of whether or not to respond. In telephony manners are everything. While in commercial television manners are nothing. If you have a receiver you merely plug in to the possibility of a signal, which may or may not be there and which you cannot modify except in the trivial manner of switching to a nearly identical transmission or in a decisive but final manner by switching off. Choice is in the hands of the sender.

Now while this asymmetry is not inherent in the technology, it has become so normative for the medium that it forms the all pervasive and invisible background of all video. This may not be so dramatically manifested in most art work video, but that's because most art works have very equivocal relations to the notion of communication and are, like industry, producer dominated. Yet it has a formidable effect on all attempts at interactive video, which operates primarily in reaction to this norm. In this sense the social structure of the medium is a matrix that defines the formal properties of the medium—since it limits the possibilities of a video communication genre—and these limits then become the target against which any number of artists have aimed their works. What else could Ira Schneider have had in mind about the 1969 piece *Wipe-Cycle* he devised with Frank Gillette:

> The most important thing was the notion of information presentation, and the notion of the integration of the audience into the information. One sees oneself exiting from the elevator. If one stands there for 8 seconds, one sees oneself entering the gallery from the elevator again. Now at the same time one is apt to be seeing oneself standing there watching *Wipe-Cycle.* You can watch yourself live watching yourself 8 seconds ago, watching yourself 16 seconds ago, *eventually feeling free enough to interact with this matrix, realizing one's own potential as an actor.*[3] [my italics]

What is attempted is the conversion (liberation) of an audience (receiver) into an actor (transmitter), which Schneider and Gillette must have hoped to accomplish by neutralizing as much as possible the acts of "taking" and electronic transmission. If they failed to accomplish this, they were hardly alone in their failure, which seems to have been the fate of just about every interactive art work employing significantly technological means. Apparently, the social and economic distribution of technological resources in this culture has a nearly determining effect on the semiotics of technological resources. More concretely, an expensive video camera and transmission system switched-on and ready for use don't lose their peculiar prestigious properties just because an artist may make them available under special circumstances for casual use to an otherwise passive public. In fact, this kind of interactive video situation almost invariably begins by intimidating an unprepared audience, which has already been indoctrinated about the amount of preparedness (professionalism) the video camera deserves, regardless of the trivial nature of television professionalism, which is not measured by competence (as in the elegant relation of ends to means) but by the amount of money notably expended on this preparation. Yet while the most fundamental property of television is its social organization, this is manifested most clearly in its money metric, which applies to every aspect of the medium, determining the tempo of its representations and the style of the performances, as well as the visual syntax of its editing. The money metric has also played a determining role in neutralizing what is usually considered the most markedly distinctive feature of the medium: the capacity for instantaneous transmission.

In principle, television seemed to combine the photographic reproduction capacities of the camera, the motion capabilities of film, and the instantaneous transmission properties of the telephone. But just as the photographic reproduction capacity of the camera is essentially equivocal and mainly significant as mythology, so is the fabled instantaneity of television essentially a rumor, that combines with photographic duplicity to produce a quasi-recording medium the main feature of which is unlikeliness in relation to any notion of reality. The history of the industry is very instructive in respect of this remarkable outcome.

In the beginning television made widespread use of live broadcasting both for transmitting instant news of events that were elapsing in real time and for more or less well-rehearsed studio performances; and some of the most interesting events recorded by media were the result of the unpredictability of instantaneous transmission. Spokesmen for the industry never failed to call attention to this feature of instantaneity, and as late as 1968, a standard handbook for television direction and production by Stasheff and Bretz asserts:

> Perhaps the most distinctive function of television is its ability to show distant events at the moment when they are taking place. The Kefauver hearings, with a close-up of the hands of gangster Frank Costello; the Army-McCarthy hearings; the complete coverage of the orbital shots; the presidential nominating conventions; the Great Debates of 1960; the live transmissions from Europe and Japan via satellite—this is television doing what no other medium can do.[4]

Yet the same handbook casually points out a few pages later that between 1947 and 1957, kine-recordings, films taken directly from the TV screen, were in constant and heavy use, especially for delayed broadcast of East Coast programs on the West Coast, in spite of the much poorer image quality of the kines, and that by 1961 virtually all television dramatic programs were being produced on film. There were, apparently, from the industry's standpoint great inconveniences in instantaneous transmission. The most obvious of these was that at the same instant of time the life cycles of New York and Los Angeles are separated by three full hours, and since the day for the industry is metrically divided into prime and non-prime viewing time, in accordance with whether more or less viewers may be sold to the advertisers, the money value of instantaneous transmission is inversely related in a complicated way to the temporal distance of transmission. But this was only the most obvious manner in which the money metric worked to eliminate instantaneity. A more basic conflict between the structure of the industry and the possibility of instantaneity is the inevitable relationship between instantaneity and unpredictability.

Any series of events that is unfolding for the first time, or in a new way, or with unanticipated intensity or duration threatens to overrun or elude the framing conventions of the recording artists (the cameramen and directors). This element of surprise is always in conflict with the image of smoothness, that has the semiotic function of marking the producer's competence by emphasizing his mastery and control, his grasp of events. The signs of unpredictability and surprise are discontinuities and ragged edges that mark the boundaries of that competence by puncturing or lacerating that grasp. The image of smoothness depends always upon the appearance of the unimpeded forward course of the producer's intention, of facility, which means that there must be no doubt in the viewer's mind that what is transmitted is what the transmitter wants to transmit. And the only ways to achieve this were through a) repeated preparation of the events, b) very careful selection of highly predictable events, c) or deletion of unexpected and undesirable aspects of events, which meant editing a recorded version of these events. Video tape came in in 1956, and at the beginning Ampex was taping the Douglas Edwards newscasts and, not much later, the stage presentations of *Playhouse 90:* once again according to Stasheff and Bretz:

> ...by 1957 a new TV revolution was under way. Undistinguishable from live TV on the home receiver, video tape quickly replaced most of the kine-recording done by the TV networks. Not only did the stations put out a better picture, but the savings were tremendous.... Live production, video-tape recording of live production, kine-recording, and film began to assume complementary roles in the pattern of TV production. Video-tape recording, by 1961 became so commonplace that the true live production—reaching the home at the moment of its origination—was a rarity limited largely to sports and special events. *The live production on video tape, though delayed in reaching the home by a few hours or a few days, was generally accepted as actual live television by the average viewer.*[5] [my italics]

Yet this did not place television in the same position as film, which from its origins appeared to be situated squarely in the domain of illusion. Film, after all, has made very few and very insubstantial claims to facticity. Amet's bathtub battle of Santiago Bay may have convinced Spanish military historians of its authenticity, but that was back in 1897 before the movie palaces together with the movie makers

dispelled any illusion of potential facticity. Flaherty looks as clearly fictional as Melies now. But a genre that is marked "fictional" doesn't raise issues of truth and falsehood, and television never ceases to raise these issues. The social uses of television continually force the issue of "truth" to the center of attention. A President goes on television to declare his "honesty," a minister announces his "intentions," the evening news reports "what is being done to curb the inflation." The medium maintains a continual assertion that it can and is providing an adequate representation of reality, while everyone's experience continually denies it. Moreover the industry exhibits a persistent positive tropism toward the appearance of the spontaneous and unrehearsed event in its perpetually recurring panel shows and quiz programs and in the apparently casual format of its late evening news shows. According to Stasheff and Bretz:

> ...the television audience will not only accept, but even enjoy, a production error or even a comedian who blows his lines and admits it or who asks his straight man to feed him a cue once again so that he can make another try at getting the gag to come out right. This leniency on the part of the audience is caused by the increased feeling of spontaneity and immediacy which minor crises create. The audience loves to admire the adroitness with which the performer "pulls himself out of a jam."[6]

The industry wishes or feels obligated to maintain the illusion of immediacy, which it defines rather precisely as "the *feeling* that what one sees on the TV screen is living and actual reality, at that very moment taking place."[7] The perfection of videotape made possible the careful manipulation and selective presentation of desirable "errors" and "minor crises" as marks of spontaneity, which became as equivocal in their implications as the drips and blots of third-generation Abstract Expressionists. It's not that you couldn't see the Los Angeles police department's tactical assault squad in real time, in full living color, in your own living room, leveling a small section of the city in search of three or four suspected criminals, but that what you would see couldn't be certainly discriminated from a carefully edited videotape screened three hours later. So what television provides video with is a tradition not of falseness, which would be a kind of guarantee of at least a certain negative reliability, but of a profoundly menacing equivocation and mannerism, determining a species of unlikeliness.

At first glance artist's video seems to be defined by the total absence of any of the features that define television. But this apparent lack of relation is in fact a very definite and predictable inverse relation. If we temporarily ignore the subfamily of installation pieces, which are actually quite diverse among themselves but nevertheless constitute a single genre, the most striking contrast between video pieces and television is in relation to time. It may not be quite hip to say so without qualification, but it is a commonplace to describe artists' videotapes as "boring" or "long," even when one feels that this in no way invalidates or dishonors the tapes in question (viz. Bruce Boice's comment that Lynda Benglis's video is "boring, interesting and funny";[8] or Richard Serra's own videotape *Prisoners' Dilemma,* where one character advises another that he may have to spend two hours in the basement of the Castelli Gallery, which is "twice as long as the average boring videotape.") This perceived quality of being boring or long has little to do with the actual length of the tapes. It has much more

to do with the attitude of just about all the artists using video to the task at hand. John Baldessari has a tape called *Some Words I Mispronounce.* He turns to a blackboard and writes:

1. poor	4. Beelzebub
2. cask	5. bough
3. bade	6. sword

As soon as he completes the "d" of "sword" the tape is over. Running time is under a minute. It feels amazingly short. But it is longer than most commercials.

Robert Morris's *Exchange,* a series of verbal meditations on exchanges of information, collaborations and interferences with a woman, accompanied by a variety of images taped and retaped from other tapes and photographs for the most part as indefinite and suggestive as the discourse, goes on till it arrives at a single distinct and comic story of not getting to see the Gattamelata, after which the tape trails off in a more or less leisurely fashion. Running time forty-three minutes. Television has many programs that are much longer. The two artists' tapes are very different. Baldessari's is a routine, explicitly defined from the outset and carried out deadpan to its swift conclusion. *Exchange* is a typical member of what is by now a well-defined genre of artist narrative, essentially an extended voiceover in a carefully framed literary style that seeks its end intuitively in the exhaustion of its mild narrative energy. But they both have the same attitude toward time: the work ends whenever its intention is accomplished. The time is inherent time, the time required for the task at hand. The work is "boring," as Les Levine remarked, "if you demand that it be something else. If you demand that it be itself then it is not boring."[9] Which is not to say that the videotapes may not be uninteresting. Whether they are interesting or not is largely a matter of judging the value of the task at hand, and this could hardly be the issue for people who can look with equanimity at what hangs on the wall in the most distinguished galleries. For whatever we think of the videotapes of Morris, or Sonnier, or Serra, they are certainly not inferior to whatever else they put in the gallery. Levine is right. Videotapes are boring if you demand that they be something else. But they're not judged boring by comparison with paintings or sculpture, they're judged boring in comparison with television, which for the last twenty years has set the standard of video time.

But the time standard of television is based firmly on the social and economic nature of the industry itself and has nothing whatever to do with the absolute technical and phenomenological possibilities of visual representation by cathode ray tube. For television, time has an absolute existence independent of any imagery that may or may not be transmitted over its well-defended airwaves and cables. It is television's only solid, a tangible commodity that is precisely divisible into further and further subdivisible homogeneous units, the smallest quantum of which is measured by the smallest segment that could be purchased by a potential advertiser, which is itself defined by the minimum particle required to isolate a salable product from among a variable number of equivalent alternatives. The smallest salable piece turns out to be the ten-second spot, and all television is assembled from it.

But the social conventions of television dictate a code of behavior according to which the transmitter must assume two apparently different roles in transmission. In one he must appear to address the viewer on the station's behalf as entertainer; in the other on the sponsor's behalf as salesman. The rules of the game, which are legally codified, prescribe a sharp demarcation between the roles, and the industry makes a great show of marking off the boundaries between its two types of performances—the programs and the commercials. At their extremes of hard-sell and soft-show, one might suppose that the stylistic features of the two roles would be sufficient to distinguish them, but the extremes are rare, the social function of the roles, not so distinct, and the stylistic features seldom provide sufficient separation. Since the industry's most tangible presentation is metrically divisible time, the industry seems to mark the separation emphatically by assigning the two roles different time signatures. The commercial is built on a scale of the minute out of multiple ten-second units. It comes in four common sizes—10, 30, 60 and 120 seconds—of which the thirty-second slot is by far the commonest. The program is built on the scale of the hour out of truncated and hinged fifteen-minute units that are also commonly assembled in four sizes—15, 30, 60 and 120 minutes—of which the half-hour program is the commonest, though the hour length is usual for important programs, two hours quite frequent for Specials and feature films, and fifteen minutes not entirely a rarity for Commentary. Television inherited the split roles and the two time signatures from radio, as well as the habit of alternating them in regularly recurrent intervals, which creates the arbitrary appearing, mechanical segmentation of both media's presentations. But television carried this mechanical segmentation to a new extreme and presented it in such a novel way, through a special combination of its own peculiar technology and production conventions, that television time in spite of structural similarity with radio time has an entirely different appearance from it, bearing the relationship to it of an electronically driven, digital counter to a spring driven, hand-wound alarmclock.

Television achieved its extreme segmentation of transmission time mainly through the intense development of multiple sponsorship. Old radio programs, from the 1930s and 1940s tended to have a single sponsor. *The Lone Ranger* was sponsored for years by Silvercup bread, *Ma Perkins* by Oxydol, *Uncle Don* by Ovaltine, and these sponsors would reappear regularly at the beginning, middle and end of each program with pretty much the same commercial pitch. This pattern continued by and large into the early days of television, with *Hallmark Theater, The Kraft Playhouse* and so on. But current television practice is generally quite different. A half-hour program might have something like six minutes of commercial fitted to it in three two-minute blocks at the beginning, middle and end of the program. But these six minutes of commercial time might promote the commodities of twelve different sponsors, or twelve different commodities of some smaller number of sponsoring agencies. The commodities could be nearly anything—a car, a cruise, a furniture polish, a breakfast food, a funeral service, a scent for men, a cure for smoking, an ice show, an x-rated movie, or a politician. In principle they could apply to nearly any aspect of human life and be presented in any order, with

strategies of advocacy more various than the commodities themselves. In practice the range of commodity and styles of advocacy are somewhat more limited, but the fact remains that in half an hour you might see a succession of four complete, distinct and unrelated thirty-second presentations, followed by a twelve-minute half of a presentation, followed by a one-minute presentation, one thirty-second presentation and two ten-second presentations, followed by the second and concluding half presentation (twelve minutes long), followed by yet another four unrelated thirty-second presentations. But since this would lead to bunching of two two-minute commercials into a four-minute package of commercial at every hour ending, and since viewers are supposed to want mainly to look at the programs—or because program makers are rather possessive about their own commercials and want complete credit for them—the program makers have recently developed the habit of presenting a small segment of their own program as a kind of prologue before the opening commercial, to separate it from the tail end of the preceding program, while the program makers of the preceding program may attempt to tag onto the end of their own program a small epilogue at the end of their last commercial, to affix it more securely to their own program. Meanwhile the station may itself interject a small commercial promoting itself or its future presentations. All of these additional segments—prologues, epilogues, station promotions and coming attractions—usually last no more than two minutes, are scaled to commercial time and are in their functional nature promotions for either immediately succeeding or eventually succeeding transmissions. This means that you may see upward of fourteen distinct segments of presentation in any half hour, all but two of which will be scaled to commercial time. Since commercial time is the most common signature, we could expect it to dominate the tempo of television, especially since the commercial segments constitute the only examples of integral (complete and uninterrupted) presentation in the medium. And it does, but not in the way one would generally suppose.

It is very easy to exaggerate the apparent differences between commercial time and program time by concentrating on the dramatic program. Television has many programs that share a mechanically segmented structure with the packet of commercials. The most extreme cases are the news programs, contests and the so-called talk shows. What is called "news" on television is a chain of successive, distinct and structurally unrelated narrations called "stories." These average from thirty seconds to two minutes in length, are usually presented in successions of three or four in a row, and bracketed between packets of commercial from one to two minutes long. The "full" story is built very much like a common commercial. It will usually have a ten- to thirty-second introduction narrated by an actor seen in a chest-shot, followed by a segment of film footage about one minute in length. There are alternate forms but all of them are built on exactly the same type of segmentation. The narrating actor may merely narrate (read off) the event from the same chest-shot seen against a background of one or two slides plausibly related to the event. The only continuity for the six- or seven-minute packet of programming called "news" consists of an abstract categorial designation (e.g. National) and the recurrent shots of the newsmen, actors who project some

well-defined character considered appropriate for this part of the show, such as informed concern, alert aggressiveness, world-weary moralism, or genial confidence, and so on. This tends to be more obvious in the packets designated as "sports" and "weather," where what passes for information consists of bits so small, numerous and unrelated that they come down to mere lists. These may be held together respectively by more obvious character actors like a suave ex-jock and a soft touch comic. Similarly, contest shows consist of structurally identical, separate events joined edge to edge and connected mainly by the continuous presence of the leading actor (the host). Television has also—through selection of the events themselves and manner of representation—managed to present most of its sports programs as sequences of nearly identical unrelated events. Baseball gets reduced to a succession of pitches, hits and catches, football to a succession of runs, passes and tackles, while the ensemble of events that may be unfolding lies outside the system of representation. If we count together all the programs that are constructed out of these linearly successive, distinct segments of commercial scale, the contrast between commercial and program becomes much less sharp. Moreover a closer inspection of both will show that there are really no clear stylistic distinctions between commercials and programs, because just about every genre of program appears also as commercial. Dramas, comedies, documentaries, science talks, lists, all show up in thirty- and sixty-second forms. Even their distinctive integralness can be exaggerated, because often there is a clean partition between the programmatic parts of the commercial—its dramatic or imagistic material—and the details of the pitch that specify the name of the product and where you can get it. This separation is so common that it is possible to watch three thirty-second commercials in succession with some pleasure and find it difficult to remember the name or even the nature of the commodity promoted. This is not a functional defect in the commercial, the main function of which is to produce a kind of praise poetry that will elevate to a mild prominence one member out of the general family of commodities that television promotes as a whole tribe all of its transmitting day. Poems in praise of particular princes are addressed to an audience already familiar with the tribe, and commercials are constructed to particularize an already existing interest. Nobody unconcerned with body odors will care which deodorant checks them best. It takes the whole television day to encode the positive images of smoothness, cleanliness or blandness upon which the massive marketing of deodorants and soaps depends. There is no fundamental distinction between commercial and program, there is only a difference in focus and conciseness, which gives the thirty-second commercial its appearance of much greater elegance and style. Both commercials and programs are assembled out of the same syntax: the linear succession of logically independent units of nearly equal duration. But this mechanically divisible, metrical presentation has none of the percussive or disjunctive properties of radio presentation. This is because of the conventions of camerawork and editing that television has developed to soften the shock of its basically mechanical procedures.

It is probably fair to say that the entire technology from the shape of the monitor screen to the design of the camera mounts was worked out to soften the tick of its metronome. Almost every instrument of television technique and technology seems to have the effect of a shock absorber. As in film, the television presentation is assembled out of separate shots. But these shots are very limited in type and duration. Because of the poor resolution of the television image (525 bits of information presented on photosensitive phosphors) and the normal screen size, the bread and butter shots of television are almost all subforms of what film would consider a close-up. Common shot names illustrate this—knee-shot, thigh-shot, waist-shot, bust-shot, head-shot, tight head-shot. Or else they count the number of people in the frame—two-shot, four-shot, etc. Probably primarily for this reason shot durations are very limited in range—usually from two to ten seconds—and very predictable in function and type. The two- to three-second shot is almost always a reaction-shot or a transition detail in a narrative, so it will usually be a head-shot or detail of some activity. Distant shots of moving cars, or whatever, will usually run seven to ten seconds, like action in general. Shots of a second and under are very rare and only used for special occasions, but distinct shots over twenty seconds are practically nonexistent. "Distinct" because television's camera conventions include a cameraman who is trained to act like an anti-aircraft gunner, constantly making minute adjustments of the camera loosening up a bit here, tightening up there, gently panning and trucking in a nearly imperceptible manner to keep the target on some imaginary pair of crosshairs. These endless, silken adjustments, encouraged and sometimes specifically called for by the director, and usually built into the cameraman's training, tend to blur the edges of what the film director would normally consider a shot. To this we can add the widespread use of fade-ins and fade-outs and dissolves to effect temporal and spatial transitions, and the directors' regular habit of cutting on movement to cushion the switch from one camera to another. This whole arsenal of techniques has a single function—to soften all shocks of transition. Naturally the different apparent functions of various genres of program or commercial will alter the degree of softening, and a news program will maintain a sense of urgency through its use of cuts, soft though they may be, while the soap opera constantly melts together its various close shots with liquid adjustment, and blends scene to scene in recurrent dissolves and fades. This ceaseless softening combines with the regular segmentation to transform the metronomic tick-tock of the transmission into the silent succession of numbers of a digital clock.

Because of the television industry's special aesthetic of time and the electronics industry's primary adaptation of the technology to the needs and desires of television, the appearance of an art-world video had to wait for the electronics industry to attempt to expand the market for its technology into special institutional and consumer domains. The basic tool kit of artists' video is the Portapak with its small, mobile camera and one-half-inch black and white videotape recorder that can accommodate nothing larger than thirty-minute tapes. Put together with a small monitor and perhaps an additional microphone, the whole operation costs something in the vicinity of $2000—a bit less than a cheap car and a bit more than a good stereo system. This is the fundamental unit, but it allows no editing whatever. The most minimal editing—edge to edge assembling of tapes into units larger than thirty

minutes—requires access to at least another videotape recorder with a built-in editing facility, which means at least the investment of another $1200. This is a primitive editing capacity, but increases the unit cost by 50 percent to about $3000. Yet precision editing and smoothness are still out of the question. Unlike film, where editing is a scissors and paste job anyone can do with very little equipment, and where you can sit in a small room and shave pieces of film down to the half frame with no great difficulty, video pictures have to be edited electronically by assembling image sequences from some source or sources in the desired order on the tape of a second machine. The images are electronically marked off from each other by an electronic signal recurring (in the U.S.) thirty times a second. If you want to place one sequence of images right after another that you've already recorded onto the second tape, you have to join the front edge of the first new frame to the final edge of the other, which means that motors of both machines have to be synchronized to the thirtieth of a second and that there must be a way of reading off each frame edge to assure that the two recorded sequences are in phase with each other. Half-inch equipment is not designed to do this, and the alignment of frame edge with frame edge is a matter of accident.

Alignment of a particular frame edge with a particular frame edge is out of the question. If the frame edges don't come together the tape is marked by a characteristic momentary breakup or instability of the image. You may or may not mind this, but it's the distinctive mark of this type of editing. Since this is absolutely unlike television editing, it carries its special mark of homemade or cheap or unfinicky or direct or honest. But the dominance of television aesthetics over anything seen on a TV screen makes this rather casual punctuation mark very emphatic and loaded with either positive or negative value. An installation with synchronized, multiple cameras, with capabilities for switching through cutting, fading and dissolving, and some few special effects like black and white reversal will cost somewhere in the $10,000 range, provided you stick to black and white and half-inch equipment. This is only a minor increase in editing control and a cost increase of one order of magnitude. If you want reliably smooth edits that will allow you to join predictably an edge to an edge, without specifying which edge, you will need access to an installation whose cost begins at around $100,000. One major art gallery has a reduced form of such a facility that permits this sort of editing, which costs about half that. Again we have an increase of control that is nearly minimal and a cost increase of another order of magnitude. Some artists have solved this problem by obtaining occasional access to institutions possessing this kind of installation, but usually this takes complete editing control out of the hands of most artists. There are also ways of adapting the one-inch system to precisionist frame-for-frame capacity, but that requires the investment of several thousand dollars more. A rule of thumb might specify that each increase in editing capacity represents an order of magnitude increase in cost. Color is still another special problem. Though it is hardly necessary, and possibly a great drawback in the sensible use of video for most artists' purposes (viz. Sonnier's pointless color work), it is by now television's common form and has certain normative marks associated with it. To use black and white is a marked move, regardless of what the mark may be construed to mean. So, many artists will seek color for mere neutrality. But it comes at a price. There are bargain basement color systems, wonderfully cheesy in appearance, but the most common system is the three-quarter-inch cassette ensemble, which together with camera, videotape recorder and monitor goes at about $10,000. If the Portapak is the Volkswagen, this is the Porsche of individual artists' video. For editing control the system of escalation in color runs parallel to black and white. The model of ultimate refinement and control is the television industry's two-inch system, and since that's what you see in action in any motel over the TV set, interesting or not, everyone takes it for the state of the art.

These conditions may not seem promising, but artists are as good at surviving as cockroaches, and they've developed three basic strategies for action. They can take the lack of technical refinements as a given and explore the theater of poverty. They can beg, borrow or steal access to technical wealth and explore the ambiguous role of the poor relation, the unwelcome guest, the court jester, the sycophant, or the spy. This isn't a common solution. The studios don't make their facilities available so readily. But it includes works done by Allan Kaprow, Peter Campus, Les Levine, Nam June Paik and numerous others. Artists can also raid the technology as a set of found objects or instruments with phenomenological implications in installation pieces. There are numerous examples from the work of Peter Campus, Dan Graham, Nam June Paik, Frank Gillette, etc. To a great extent the significance of all types of video art derives from its stance with respect to some aspect of television, which is itself profoundly related to the present state of our culture. In this way video art embarks on a curiously mediated but serious critique of the culture. And this reference to television, and through it to the culture, is not dependent on whether or not the artist sees the work in relation to television. The relation between television and video is created by the shared technologies and conditions of viewing, in the same way the relation of movies to underground film is created by the shared conditions of cinema. Nevertheless, an artist may exploit the relation very knowingly and may choose any aspect of the relation for attack.

If Nancy Holt's *Underscan* is an innocent masterpiece that narrates in its toneless voice a terrifying, impoverished story over a sequence of simple photographic images ruined twice over by the television raster, the co-related Benglis *Collage* and Morris *Exchange* are cunning parodies that use the cheesy video image to depreciate a filmic genre that would sensuously exploit the personal glamour of stars like Elizabeth Taylor and Richard Burton, replaced here by the mock glamour of two pseudo-celebrities in a visual soup. Holt calls into question anything that the medium has ever represented as documentary with her sheer simplicity of means, while Morris and Benglis produce a total burlesque of the public figure through the manifest absurdity of their claims.

Acconci's *Undertone* is an even more precise example of this type of burlesque. In a visual style of address exactly equivalent to the presidential address, the face-to-face camera regards The Insignificant Man making The Outrageous Confession that is as likely as not to be an Incredible Lie. Who can escape the television image of Nixon?

In Baldessari's wonderful *Inventory*, the artist presents to the camera for thirty minutes an accumulation of indiscriminate and not easily legible objects arranged in order of increasing size and accompanied by a deadpan description—only to have the sense of their relative size destroyed by the continual readjustment of the camera's focal length that is required to keep them within the frame. Who can forget Adlai Stevenson's solemn television demonstration of the "conclusive photographic evidence" of the Cuban missile sites, discriminable over the TV screen as only grey blurs?

What the artists constantly re-evoke and engage with is television's fundamental equivocation and mannerism, which may really be the distinctive feature of the medium. But they may do this from two diametrically opposed angles, either by parodying the television system and providing some amazing bubble or by offering to demonstrate how, with virtually no resources, they can do all the worthwhile things that television should do or could do in principle and has never yet done and never will do.

Terry Fox's *Children's Tapes* exhibit nothing more nor less than the simple laws of the physical world in terms of small common objects—a spoon, a cup, an ice cube, a piece of cloth. They make use of a single camera, adjusted only enough to get the objects and events into the frame, and no edits. The hands crumple a spoon handle, place an ice cube in it over a small piece of cloth, balance it at the neck over the rim of a cup. You watch. It takes how long for you to figure out that the ice cube will melt? That the cloth will absorb the water. That the balance will be upset. But which way? Will the water absorbed into the cloth be drawn further from the fulcrum and increase the downward moment on the ice cube side? Or will the water dripping from the spoon reduce the downward moment and send the spoon toppling into the cup? You watch as though waiting for an explosion. It takes minutes to come and you feel relieved. It has the form of drama. You'll never see anything like it on educational television or any other television. It takes too much time, intelligence and intensity of attention to watch—except on video. There are, I believe, twenty-two of them. They have the brilliance of still-life and the intelligence of a powerful didactic art. But it is also a critique of means. Other works similar in this respect of means are Richard Serra's *Prisoners' Dilemma* and Eleanor Antin's *The Ballerina and the Bum*.

The Serra piece shamelessly adapts a casual stage skit and a contest show format to illustrate hilariously and with absolute simplicity a moral-logical dilemma with grave implications for human action. The problem is apparently simple. There are two prisoners, A and B. Each is offered a chance to betray the other and go free—but here is the first catch—provided the other refuses to betray him. In the event that this happens the prisoner who refuses to betray will receive the maximum sentence—this is catch 2. The other alternatives are that both prisoners will refuse to betray each other; this will get both prisoners the second lightest penalty; or that both prisoners will attempt to betray each other, which will get each prisoner the second gravest penalty. On the face of it we have a straightforward 2 x 4 matrix with four outcomes for each player, but all the outcomes are linked pairs: you go free only if he gets life imprisonment and he goes free only if you get life imprisonment; you both get away with two years' imprisonment if you both hold out against betrayal; you both get ten years' imprisonment if you both try betrayal. If each player plays the game as a zero-sum game for his own advantage, he will inspect the reward columns and come to the single conclusion that the worst possible outcome is life imprisonment, which can only happen if he refuses to betray. This prevents the other player from screwing him and leaves the original player the chance of screwing his opponent. Since both players—regarded as unrelated individuals who will consider their own individual advantage—will both play to minimize their loss, they will each play to cut their losses and inevitably come out with the next to worst payoff—ten years in prison. There is no way to win and no way to play for mutual non-betrayal because failure to betray always risks total loss. But the video piece is more brilliant than that. It sets up two precise illustrations—comic, yes; casual, yes—but elegant in the way it demonstrates that any two unrelated prisoners—say a pair of suspected criminals picked up in the street—will inevitably betray each other and take the consequences. But any two prisoners who have a real community bond between them have no choice but to play for non-betrayal, because they must consider the value of the outcome in terms of its value for both players. Obviously, the differences in negative weights assigned to the penalties will work differently in deciding the outcome. Still, nothing in the world of this low-budget game could make Leo Castelli betray Bruce Boice in public. This low-budget marker calls up beautiful improvisational acting from all of the players and loose styles from all of the collaborators in this group piece. The logical structuring of the piece owes a great deal to Robert Bell, who occupies a role somewhere between script-writer and director, and to all of the actors, whose improvisatory performances contribute markedly to the final outcome of the piece, which must be considered a community venture with Richard Serra assuming the producer's role. This piece is also of a sort that will never appear on television and has the force of a parable.

Antin's *Ballerina and the Bum,* another low-budget job, with single Portapak camera and two improvising actors, declares itself, from its five-minute opening shot, against television, time and money. The camera changes position only if it has to, to keep something in view, pans once along three cars of a freight train, to count them, moves inside the car. The mike has no windscreen. The sounds of the world of 1974—cars, airplanes, children and chickens—intermittently penetrate the film style illusion of the image of a Sylphides-costumed, New York-accented ballerina "from the sticks" and a twenty-five year-old grizzled old bum on the way to the big city. Nothing happens but what they say and do. She practices ballet, sets up light housekeeping in the boxcar, they daydream of success, he cooks some beans, she eats them, the train goes nowhere. Everything else is moving—cars, planes and other trains. A whole Chaplin movie for the price of a good dub.

Other successful examples of this low-budget strategy are Andy Mann's *One-Eyed Bum* and Ira Schneider and Beryl Korot's *4th of July in Saugerties,* which bring to bear the video of limited means upon documentary as a

kind of artist's reminder of the ambiguities of "honesty" and "simplicity." It is no accident that the best of these works have, at least in part, a didactic and moral element behind them and are "exemplary." And even the tapes that are not specifically presented in an exemplary mode become exemplary in their fundamental disdain for television time.

But the theater of poverty isn't the only way. Peter Campus somehow infiltrated WGBH-TV, Boston, to produce a single deadly piece precisely aimed through their expensive equipment. A man holding a photograph, seemingly of himself. You see him set fire to it and watch it burn from all four sides. Gradually you notice that the photograph is breathing, its eyes are blinking. This is the image of television.

FOOTNOTES

1. Judson Rosenbush, ed. *Frank Gillette Video: Process and Metaprocess.* Essay by Frank Gillette, interview by Willoughby Sharp. (Syracuse, N.Y.: Everson Museum of Art, 1973), p. 21.

2. Hollis Frampton, "The Withering Away of the State of Art," *Artforum* (Dec. 1974): 50.

3. Jud Yalkut, "TV As a Creative Medium at the Howard Wise Gallery," *Arts Magazine* (Sept. 1961): 21.

4. Edward Stasheff and Rudy Bretz, *The Television Program: Its Writing, Direction and Production.* (New York: A. A. Wyn, 1951), p. 3.

5. Ibid., p. 6.

6. Ibid., p. 8.

7. Ibid., p. 8.

8. Bruce Boice, "Lynda Benglis at Paula Cooper Gallery," *Artforum* (May 1973): 83.

9. Les Levine "Excerpts from a Tape: 'Artistic'," *Art-Rite* (Autumn 1974):27.

DIRECTIONS IN VIDEO ART
Lizzie Borden

Videotapes by artists differ from commercial television in their means of distribution and broadcasting, even though these distinctions may eventually disappear with a wider availability of public-access channels and cable TV. At present, the economic limitations on video artists strongly affect the content of their work, for the structures and characteristics of both television and video depend upon the level of technology used. These economic considerations make it impossible to ascribe to video any essential qualities that underly its use in all circumstances. Video is, rather, a polyreferential tool which is used for many different purposes and has developed from a variety of sources.

Videotapes by artists have both art and non-art histories. In their production, the traditions of music, painting, sculpture, environmental work, performance, Happenings, and Fluxus are combined with cybernetics, computer programming, and behavioral science, as well as with the broader cultural influences that have affected commercial TV: film, radio broadcasting, and theater. Many of the editing habits and narrative structures of film have been carried over into video and TV with the creation of electronic equivalents for wipes, fades, and superimpositions. The physical layout and audiometrics of the radio studio, drawn from theater design, have set precedents for the TV studio, as, for example, in the placement of the microphones and the control room. Video by artists has also been greatly influenced by TV style and genre—talk show, commercial, quiz program, news report, direct address, and documentary.

In the past decade, video by artists has developed in at least three major directions: abstraction, representation, and closed-circuit environments. The first, abstract video, might more appropriately be called reflexive or self-referential video. In reflexive video

Les Levine *Contact: A Cybernetic Sculpture* 1969

imagery is artificially created by the manipulation of the TV frequency, and comes directly from the technological processes inherent in television and its systems. Frequently, reflexive video requires a matrix of monitors regulated by a multi-channel switching system which is sometimes programmed by a computer "brain." Another use of video is more narrative or representational. It is mimetic of the external world even when it incorporates feedback which, in video, is audiovisual interference created by the equipment itself and added, with a few micro-seconds delay, to the outgoing signals, thereby amplifying the present-time output with past-time output. Still another use of video has been in the creation of a closed-circuit environment, a space dominated by at least one video camera and monitor. Unlike reflexive video, video in a closed-circuit environment does not operate independently from its viewers, but works with their perception of real and video spaces as well as with their physical and psychological dislocations from familiar means of orientation. This aspect of video is sometimes explored in video performance, where the relation between the audience and the performer may be altered through the medium of television. Since all of these types of video involve different modes of temporality and spatial extension, the ways in which they are presented and read are vastly dissimilar.

Artists who work with the technology of video have often demonstrated a religious fervor for the intricacies of their hardware. They are the media-freaks who have romantically identified themselves with the machine. The content of their work is determined both by the process of video and the context or situation in which it is made. The image, as such, has no value apart from the matrix. This attitude, which leads the artists to metaphors for the computer brain based on the human brain, is reminiscent of the ideas of both Marshall McLuhan and the cyberneticist Norbert Weiner in the way it points up similarities between electronics and physiology. Weiner's argument centered on the similarity in the means of control and communication in the animal and the machine: "the binary code of today's computer has its origin in the 'all or nothing' character of our Neuron synapses, which are simply ON or simply OFF."[1]

Nam June Paik was one of the first artists to experiment with the technological processes of video. Paik's experimental work in television grew out of his study of electronic music with Karlheinz Stockhausen in Cologne during the late fifties. His work was also influenced by his involvement with Fluxus and Happenings as well as by the ideas of Weiner, McLuhan, and the composer John Cage. Paik's work shares with Happenings their operatic impetus and constant metamorphosis, where the line between art and life was kept fluid, the sources of themes and materials were non-art situations, time was variable and discontinuous, and events occurred only once. The blurring of distinctions between art forms and life also characterized Fluxus, an iconoclastic movement organized in Germany by George Macunias in the early sixties, which included concerts, events, and performances by artists such as George Brecht, Dick Higgins, La Monte Young, and Paik. Fluxus operated in the interstices between painting, sculpture, music, dance, theater, and poetry and its products were regarded as truly "inter-media" rather than "mixed media."[2] John Cage was a catalyst in the thinking of Fluxus artists in that their music consisted of simple events in which ordinary or chance sounds were incorporated. Paik's work drew from Cage's in the use of structuring devices such as indeterminacy which allows for improvisation.

From 1963, Paik "prepared" TVs in the way that the composer David Tudor doctored up pianos: he placed electromagnets on top of TV sets to distort the broadcast signal of commercial TV. His early interest in transforming music by TV also informed a witty work from 1969, *TV Bra for Living Sculpture,* in which the sound of Charlotte Moorman's cello modulated the picture on her TV bra. Paik also played on TVs with wave-form generators, amplifiers, and tape recorders. His simultaneous use of many monitors demonstrated, even more than did the quickly changing content of commercial programs, McLuhan's point about the "mosaic" of TV experience, namely, that many separate threads of perception are simultaneously perceived.

The prepared TVs and work on various video components beginning in 1955 led Paik to the invention of the video synthesizer in 1970 in collaboration with the engineer Shuya Abe. Video synthesizing is a way of combining two or more elements in order to project a composite picture. One of the limitations of video synthesizing for most artists is that the range of shapes which can be produced and the speed of the synthesizer in producing them are determined by the technical means available to the artist, and all too often this is, in turn, limited by the amount of money available. For example, one reason why many images look psychedelic is purely economic: it is easier, and therefore less expensive, to make different-sized images appear in series and change symmetrically than it is to create a different image at each scan. Paik himself has surmounted these limitations, however, because his frequent position as Artist in Residence at WNET-TV Laboratory in New York and at WGBH-TV in Boston has given him access to the full range of technical capabilities available in these network studios and thereby allowed him to

apply his profound understanding of electronics to the creation of masterful works. Paik too has made visionary claims about the possibilities of TV synthesizers. In regard to his color synthesizer of 1970, he has written:

> In the long-ranged future, such a versatile color synthesizer will become a standard equipment like today's Hammond organ, or Moog synthesizer in the musical field....
>
> 1) TV-tranquilizer....the tranquilizing "groovy" TV will be an important function of future TV, like today's mood music....
> 2) Enormous enrichment of background scenery of music programs or talkshows, combined with sharp reduction in the production cost....Traditional psychedelic light show cannot compete with electronic color synthesizer....
> 3) This will provide valuable experiments for EVR [Electronic Video Recording], which would be aimed for more sophisticated or educational layer of consumer.[3]

In a more concrete vein, Paik drew up a report dealing with the expansion of education possible in a global university. Among his suggestions was the production of video records to capture the presence of great thinkers, and videotapes of musical performances in which one instrument or voice has been omitted so that it could later be supplied by the student, thus giving him the simulated experience of playing or singing with a full orchestra.

While Paik has written about the use of video to store information, many artists have developed video works whose aesthetic organization has grown out of information theory. Frank Gillette, whose art and writing have been influenced by cybernetics, created an elaborate and highly developed video matrix in 1974. Called *Track/Trace,* it manipulates information by presenting it through a series of time delays.

Three television cameras record and transmit the contents of the gallery to a matrix of fifteen television monitors arranged in the face of a tetrahedron. A switcher changes images every 8 seconds. One television monitor is mounted at the apex, two televisions are mounted on the second row down, three on the third, four on the fourth, and five on the fifth.

A television camera pointed at the observer feeds a "live" real-time image into the single, apex monitor. The image is delayed three seconds and then replayed on the second row. It is then delayed an additional three seconds (a total of six seconds) and replayed on the third row. The process continues until the bottom, or fifth row, where the original image is replayed twelve seconds after it appeared on the top monitor. These images, and those from two other television monitors, are alternated on the monitors. All fifteen monitors feed back their content simultaneously.[4]

In an earlier piece, *Wipe Cycle*, made in collaboration with Ira Schneider in 1969, Gillette also attempted, as Schneider has noted, to "integrate the audience into the information. It was a live feedback system which enabled the viewer standing within its environment to see himself not only now in time and space, but also eight seconds ago and sixteen seconds ago. In addition he saw standard broadcast images alternating with his own delayed/live image. And also collage-type programed tapes, ranging from a shot of the earth, to outer space, to cows grazing, and a 'skin flick' bathtub scene."[5] As an outgrowth of a 1968 work called *Iris*, Les Levine constructed, in 1969, *Contact*, a video matrix which also engaged the spectator. The piece was an eight-foot high sculpture bank of nine TV monitors on either side, and eight TV cameras with different lenses set at different angles. Viewers saw themselves in nine different colors in close-up, medium range, and long range on monitors whose screens are each covered with a different colored acrylic gel.

Since the closed-circuit systems in these works are multi-channeled, the viewer is forced to perceive many events simultaneously. The complexity of the information presented counteracts any tendency toward a single reading. It compels the viewer to focus and refocus on a constantly changing field. It has often been suggested that this kind of perception parallels the scanning and focusing process that takes place in normal vision which operates at the "process level":

> A process level analysis of the art experience is concerned with art as a process of perception, a way of experiencing, how one sees rather than what one sees....The process level affirms direct, sensory perception....[6]

However, it seems that the video process they describe operates at the level of the video system's mechanism rather than at the core of the viewer's perception. Moreover, while Gillette has asserted that "the viewer becomes the information"[7] and Levine that his work "synthesizes man and his technology,"[8] it seems that the spectator is merely the agent for the realization of the video's program; whether it involves time delays, mixes, distortions, or wipes is immaterial. Instead of creating an interaction between the spectator and the system, these programs merely objectify and manipulate the viewer. It is not true that the viewer simultaneously experiences himself at different times or in different places, for by the time he recognizes his image, his attention has shifted from himself to the program. Consequently, these systems are sometimes illustrations of the ideas about information theory for which they are models. They are very close to traditional sculpture in that they are three-dimensional objects, but they have the added dimension of self-fulfillment as their programs play out their permutations through time. Only in more reciprocal systems where there is interaction between the viewer and his situation could there be a real investigation of perceptual intake and feedback.

In contrast to this kind of video art, which relies heavily for its conception on the equipment used and is influenced by the structuring techniques of other media (such as sound-delay in music and the mechanics of computer programming), single-monitor videotape takes its content as well as its structure from traditional art forms and cultural genre. Before coming into its own as a medium, video had been used as a means of presenting other media. For example, it documented public and private performances and extended the photographic records of Conceptual, Body, and Earth Art. Through broadcasting, video provided a way of making this art and its ideas available to a larger audience.

At the same time that artists began to use video for documentation, a series of experimental Artist-in-Residence programs, funded by The Rockefeller Foundation, was established in 1967 at WGBH-TV in Boston, WNET-TV in New York, and at KQED-TV in San Francisco. Thus broadcast television made the ideas of artists available to a wider audience. In the following year James Newman created an "open gallery" at KQED-TV, which produced a series of programs of works by sculptor Walter de Maria, choreographers Yvonne Rainer and Ann Halprin, the Living Theater, composer Terry Riley, and others. The year 1968 also marked the beginning of experimental programming at WDR in Cologne and the founding of "Fernsehgalerie Gerry Schum" in Düsseldorf. A year later *Land Art*, a documentation of earthworks by American and European artists, produced and directed by Gerry Schum, was transmitted over ARD in Germany. These projects were concerned with rethinking the economics of art in a move away from the saleable object toward the transmission of "free" ideas. This attitude was an outgrowth of the Conceptualist emphasis on the primacy of the idea

over its execution. However, this use of television only increased the audience for already known artists, who often presented non-video works, and did not introduce its audiences to new artists or programming. The format of the program itself remained submerged within the framework of commercial TV.

The availability of the Portapak, in 1968, was a more significant step toward video's becoming an independent art medium. Although a modest technological advance, the Portapak was important for artists because it is a self-sufficient and relatively inexpensive system. It was easy to document activities with the Portapak, which was preferable to film because it offers the possibility of instantaneous feedback.

The sculptor Bruce Nauman was one of the first artists to use video to document his activities. In 1967 he had been making and recording photographically works such as arrangements of flour on his studio floor which he altered every day. These pieces led to his works of 1968 in which he performed for his own pleasure. His interest in documenting his own activities made him more aware of ideas then current in music and dance. His earlier introduction to Meredith Monk as well as his exposure to the Judson dancers allowed him to see his own exercises as dance problems: "You can take any simple movement and make it into a dance just by presenting it as a dance."[9] Nauman was investigating sustained physical exertion in tasks which require great concentration, and the kinds of tensions that arise when a person tries to maintain a difficult balance or becomes fatigued. While on the East Coast in 1968, he became interested in the music of La Monte Young, Philip Glass, Terry Riley, and Steve Reich. His studio activities, sometimes dealing with rhythmic patterning, reflect the serial repetition of this music, which does away with the sense of duration while intensifying one's awareness of the moment. Nauman's interest in activities and his work with music and dance awakened public interest in these art forms, not as music or dance, but as "performance."

At first Nauman used film to document his work, but later changed to the video camera which was lighter than a film camera and could be put into various positions:

> After I had made a few films I changed to videotape, just because it was easier for me to get at the time. The camera work became a bit more important, although the camera was stationary in the first ones....the videotapes I did after those films were related, but the camera was often turned upside down, or a wide angle lens used for distortion.[10]

The camera was horizontal in *Violin Tuned D.E.A.D.*, 1969, and *Slow Angle Walk*, 1968, and upside down in *Revolving Upside Down*, 1969, and *Lip Sync*, 1969. These camera angles are frequently very expressive. In *Slow Angle Walk*, Nauman walks out of and back into camera range. His image, returning from unpredictable positions, is intensified by the horizontal plane of the camera. In *Revolving Upside Down*, occasional close-ups evoke strong emotional reactions, which are again exaggerated by the camera position.

Nauman's videotapes are an hour long, while his early films lasted only about ten minutes. Consequently, the tapes intensify the feeling that the activities they present have no beginning and no end. In later tapes, such as *Elke Allowing the Floor to Rise Up Over Her, Face Up*, 1973, the camera is in motion panning and dissolving at five-minute intervals to suggest the rhythm of passing time. In all the tapes, a certain distance is maintained between Nauman and the

audience because many of the activities are neutral and because the unusual camera angles tend to depersonalize the performer. Yet, as Nauman has said, some of the tapes evoke empathetic body responses on the part of the viewer:

> What I discovered...was that even though you set this mechanical list of things that can be done and you do them within a narrow boundary of some kind, there would be emotional responses to some just because it is a person doing that. Some things call up strong emotional responses and some don't.[11]

Another sculptor, Keith Sonnier, also moved on to videotape from performance. His first tapes, in which performers play with a few props within a static situation, are unedited chunks of video time. Sonnier plays with the ambiguity of video images. This ambiguity is exaggerated by his use of special effects such as wipes, reversals from positive to negative, and split screens. For example, in *Light Bulb and Fire*, 1970, a black "hole" or spot appears on the screen from time to time. Only later does the viewer realize that this is caused by a trick light bulb going on and off. In all of his tapes, Sonnier uses props that are keys to the processes of video. For example, the light bulb is a metaphor for the binary nature of video technology— on-off, negative-positive. He reinforces the interplay between live and video images by presenting both actual events and their electronic parallels. In *1-200*, 1972, positive-negative reversals are created actually by turning lights on and off, and technologically by means of a Special-Effects Generator, or SEG. Each of these modes of lighting can be recognized by the character of the light source: literal lighting has a precise position within the video space while electronic lighting is diffuse or varied. In the same tape, Sonnier uses panels with rectangular openings through which images can be seen, punning on the electronic creation of quadrants through special effects. Sonnier also puns in color, as, for example, in *Color Wipe*, 1973, where actual color panels are seen in relation to electronic color-keying.

Sonnier's tapes also show, rather completely, the studio spaces where they are made since he combines the images from two cameras by using an SEG. While in *Mat Key and Radio Track*, 1972, he uses two cameras to show the same thing from different perspectives, in *TV In and TV Out*, 1972, he uses two cameras to pick up and transmit different information. For the performers, Suzanne Harris and Tina Girouard, the camera plays a role in the performance and acts as a control which is sometimes psychologically loaded. In *TV In and TV Out*, Harris could not see her own video image but had microphone contact with Girouard, who could see her own image and that of Harris. Sonnier, who was in the control room giving instructions, could see and contact both performers, Girouard directly and Harris by microphone. In *Color Wipe*, Harris and Girouard operated two large, rotating, studio cameras as though they were guns, sometimes crossing each other's visual path, sometimes focusing on each other's camera-eye. In these situations, the SEG allows the visual information to be viewed simultaneously in different ways through the use of split screens and quadrants. Even though there is more than one reading of the space that unfolds with this use of cameras and microphones, the limits of the space revealed are determined by the set-up of the TV studio and the off-screen control room. In a sense, these tapes illustrate places and provide a visual means of reconstructing situations not directly portrayed.

Sonnier began to move away from in-studio performances toward work with computers that generate abstract patterns, such as the graphics-display units generally used for the animation of type and cartoons. Unlike video artists who were involved with the technology itself, Sonnier was not interested in creating his own machine, synthesizer, or matrix. In *Animation I*, 1973, he used a simple computer, called "Scanimate." Because "Scanimate" could not store information or play more than one track at a time, the tape was made in three separate steps. Sonnier's second computer tape, *Animation II*, 1974, was made on a more complex machine called "Caesar." To explore the parameters of the computer set-up, Sonnier divided the computer frame into seven parts with an input, a rotating axis, and an independent track for each. Any number of these sections could be called up, eliminated, superimposed on another, or twisted. The patterns Sonnier used included textures and colored bars. "Caesar" allowed for a more complex time than that of a linear continuum, because the computer could animate and store information to be recalled when desired. Viewers know that they are seeing only segments of tapes which are stored in their entirety in the computer's memory bank and they understand that much more time would be required to see all of each tape. Thus they have a sense of longer stretches of time than the one actually spent in watching *Animation II*.

Sonnier's computer tapes are like the video matrices of other artists in that they are limited by the capabilities of their programs, and can only illustrate the brain of the computer. However, Sonnier also feels frustrated by this one-directional nature of video output. When asked if he were interested in direct television broadcast, he replied:

> That could work if everybody had a live feedback situation, but television—and radio, most radio except for the lesser forms of radio that people aren't interested in, like Citizen's band—is still all about sending out information, and not about receiving it.[12]

Sonnier's most recent works, such as *N.Y.–L.A. Hookup,* 1974, and *Send-Receive-Send,* 1973, are telephone pieces in which the energy of sending and receiving is at both ends of a line of communication so that the audience is made a part of the structure of the piece. This form had been first investigated by Allan Kaprow in *Hello,* 1968, at WGBH-TV in Boston, which according to Kaprow "approached the medium of video as if it were a picture telephone. The telephone is so common it no longer makes any claim as 'technology' and acts therefore as a personal and social medium."[13]

Vito Acconci's early work with video also developed out of a need to document his performance activities. At first Acconci used photographs, then in 1969 film, for direct, unedited documentations. For example, in a Super-8 film of 1971, *Conversions,* he used a candle to burn the hair from around his breasts, pushed the flesh to simulate female breasts, then did exercises such as walking, running, jumping, and stretching, with his penis hidden between his legs as if he were a woman. Acconci has written of his early pieces:

> None of these films should stand alone... I should take them together: a form of justified behavior—concentration exercises, training positions, tactical attitudes (they can serve as a foundation for a course of development—an orientation toward mobility, flexibility, durability.)[14]

This comment is also appropriate to Acconci's early videotapes, a medium he used interchangeably with film. In other tapes, however, he responds to his own image on the video monitor. In *Body Works,* 1970, for example, with the camera focused on his back and using the monitor in front of him as a mirror, he lit a match and burned tufts of hair from the nape of his neck. In *Centers,* 1971, he pointed at his image in the monitor, while trying to keep his finger in the center of the screen.

Acconci moved away from the performance of physical tasks by a single person toward the psychological interchange between persons and began to use video to explore the "performance areas" that exist between people. In this work, he was influenced by contemporary writings in the field of kinesics, particularly that of Kurt Lewin and Erving Goffman. Acconci's new tapes operate on three levels of performance: the portrayal of a personal relationship, the presentation of this drama to an audience, and the study of interpersonal behavior on a larger scale. While several tapes only record live performances, tapes such as *Remote Control,* 1971, made from a performance, use video to influence the interaction between performers.

Acconci has also used video in live performance as a way of being indirectly present to the viewer. In *Claim,* 1971, a three-hour performance, he sat in the basement of 93 Grand Street, New York, blindfolded, with metal pipes and a crowbar at hand. Upstairs, next to the stairway door, a TV monitor recorded his activity for the audience, who had the choice of either watching on the monitor or going downstairs to confront Acconci and dodge his lunges at them with the crowbar. Acconci gradually worked himself into a state of violence about his possession of the territory. "I'm alone down here...I want to stay alone down here...I'll stop anyone from coming down the stairs...I've got to believe this...."

Recently, however, Acconci has been ambivalent about video performance altogether:

> I find it difficult to give the video part a reason for existence: it has to reveal something that the live performance doesn't reveal....In some earlier pieces it seemed that I put myself in isolation for the purpose of being revealed outside on the monitor. And it seems absurd: if I'm there, I might as well be really there.[15]

In his desire to change his mode of presence before the audience, Acconci began working with videotapes that create the feeling of directness and, even, exchange with the audience. The prototype of this attempt is *Undertone*, 1972, in which he is seated at the far end of a long table, facing the camera, looking down, his arms hidden under the table. He tries to convince himself that there is a girl under the table, and then that it is only himself rubbing his thighs. Then he clasps his hands together on top of the table and speaks directly to the audience at the other end of the table, implicating them in his self-coercion: "I need you to keep your place there at the end of the table....I need you to screen out my lies, filter out the lies from the real point of view." In another tape, *Command Performance*, 1973, Acconci creates a greater distance between himself and the audience. His attitude toward the audience is both seductive and antagonistic as he plays the stand-up comedian who wins people over but also makes fools of them at the same time. In these tapes, Acconci uses video as a means of presentation, while drawing from sources in popular forms of entertainment such as radio, commercial TV, and nightclub acts.

> What interests me about video is its use as a kind of home companion, it's a place for close-up. I can be face-to-face with a viewer, I can be one point in a space that includes the viewer....Maybe this would be clearer if I compared it with the way I want to use film—movie is the landscape, drift, shifting scenes....I think of movies as basically silent, whereas in video sound is the kernel.[16]

As more and more artists began to explore the medium and use its processes as content, they had to deal with video on the low level of Portapak resolution, or clarity of image, which included visual "noise," or feedback, static, etc. Many artists seized upon these elements fetishistically, as if carrying out an obligation to be "honest" to the medium. Their work was centered on their narcissistic interactions with their own images displayed on the monitor, exploited the ambiguity between first- and second-generation images, and used the infinite regressions of monitors seen on monitors. The content of this work became these characteristics themselves, because they overwhelmed the images. The quality of the picture on half-inch tape, compared with the two-inch tape of commercial TV, has always been problematical. The low resolution creates a lack of differentiation between images; landscapes become pattern and distances can't be conveyed; there is a restricted range of values, and no subtleties of lighting; the shading is often unreliable, and the imagery is often interrupted by undesired static. If these characteristics (or imperfections) are disregarded by the artist, the viewer is left with a tape on this gritty level. The lack of quality in the image is further exaggerated because the monitor is only a small object in a relatively large environment. Another quality frequently exploited as "honesty" to the medium has been the use of "real" time in video. However, the originality of this approach was undercut by Andy Warhol. His films, such as *Empire* and *Sleep*, both of 1963-64, anticipated the use of uninterrupted actual time, but were perverse in using film, a medium of spatial and temporal transport through editing, as a way of relentlessly enforcing a present-time situation. In television, on the other hand, real time actually is inherent in the medium, for what the camera sees can be immediately viewed, without the delay for processing as in film. Video is instantaneous.

Another challenge to video artists has been to develop ideas about editing that do not imitate those of film. There is no literal frame in video as there is in film, but rather visual phrasing, which is a more gestural way of reading images. The equivalent of the film-shot is the bracketing of a sequence in video. The more successful videotapes have been edited in accord with the processes of video and in such a way as to avoid overpowering any discrete images.

Joan Jonas's tape, *Vertical Roll*, 1972, uses as a structural device the vertical roll that results from the simultaneous use of two frequencies which are out of synchronization. The first is the frequency signal being sent to the set and the second is the frequency by which it is interpreted. The two are usually stabilized in TV and video and thus the image is at rest, though changing, centered on the tube. Instead of considering the roll as interference, Jonas uses the rolling picture rhythmically, creating a natural "frame" for images. This is intensified by the sound track on which she is heard banging a spoon against a mirror or clapping pieces of wood together to mark the moment when the roll strikes the bottom of the monitor, making it sound solid and material. The constancy of the banging intensifies the visual effect. Within this structure, the images seem to "roll" into view. Jonas plays with ambiguous images, odd camera angles, and technological effects such as the white traces left by the vidicon tube's reaction to light. The images are, for the most part, horizontal lines including a black band, rolling vertically off the screen, but sometimes, as she is seen to jump up and down, Jonas creates the illusion of having jumped over the roll as her actions go out of synchronization with the rhythm. The images on the tape always appear within the framework of the roll, yet are distinguishable as discrete images. The viewer of the tape suffers a disorienting perceptual illusion as the floor of the room where the tape is played seems to rise up and the monitor seems to sink into the floor. Whether or not this effect was intentional, it is a unique experience in peripheral vision, all the more remarkable as one is watching the tape on a relatively small monitor.

Another tape that uses a structuring device possible only in video is *Underscan*, 1974, by Nancy Holt. The underscanning device on the monitor is a button that compresses the picture so that the edges can be seen precisely. Holt uses two underscanned images: one caused by the button pushed halfway in, compressing the vertical sides of the picture and thereby elongating the images, and the other by the button pushed all the way in, reducing the whole picture. Holt uses this device in displaying photographs of her Aunt Ethel's house in New Bedford, Massachusetts, as she reads portions of her letters from her aunt. Each photograph is seen three times as it is subtly transformed through underscanning. The tape begins with a blank monitor seen rolling in the distance, centered in an empty black space. The camera zooms in on the monitor and the photographs begin to appear until they eventually take up all the monitor space as the soundtrack begins. The original audio-tape was played into the underscan monitor and the resultant sound retaped, so that the viewer is at one more remove from the original sound. The repetitious and coldly mechanical underscanning is in contrast to the intimate content of the letters which describe incidents from Aunt Ethel's life—sicknesses, deaths, accidents, the decay of her house—read by Holt in a voice without affect.

In a different way of turning to advantage the visual peculiarities of video, Robert Morris has pushed the images to the periphery in *Exchange*, 1973. A fictitious text is read by Stephen Koch to the accompaniment of visual images which are primarily from tapes made earlier. One recurrent sequence, which shows Morris moving up out of the frame with his back to the camera, is from Lynda Benglis's tape, *Mumble*, 1972. *Mumble* is one tape in an ongoing dialogue between Morris and Benglis in which they exchange tapes as raw material for the other's taped response. Other images in Morris's *Exchange* are of still photographs of, for example, racing cars, Carolee Schneeman as Olympia in Morris's dance *Site,* Morris on horseback, and a multi-faced picture of Benglis. The only live sequence in the tape is of Morris in a recording studio, with his back again to the camera and a photograph of Buster Keaton filling in as his alter-ego. The complex text winds around fictitious events, uses "asides" and other literary conceits, and creates the character of the narrator partly through an unembodied voice—not unlike radio. In *Exchange,* attention is focused on the soundtrack which provides more information than do the visual images. Some of the most interesting tapes by other artists have centered on a disproportioning of image and sound, which are recorded simultaneously on a single tape by video equipment. Paul Kos, for example, frequently manipulates the balance between the video image and sound; in *Mar Mar March,* 1972-73, the sound of a typewriter is distorted to resemble marching troops. Lynda Benglis also dislocates video image and sound in *Mumble* and other tapes. Certainly Ernie Kovacs mastered this technique to transform ordinary events into the art of high comedy.

Other artists have based their video presentations on models derived from commercial TV. William Wegman, for instance, borrows the straightforward, eye-to-eye, low-keyed approach of talk shows, product demonstrations, and early comedians such as Ernie Kovacs. Yet Wegman uses TV genre ironically to play with the structure of the joke in order to find out what makes something funny. He uses the format of the skit, a self-sustained unit, to put together on a single reel a series of short segments which are united by a particular strain of humor. Sometimes he personifies inanimate objects, shows his dog Man Ray's reaction to a situation, or dubs in sound to create a disparity between the soundtrack and the action. Wegman also borrows literary or visual styles from fairy tales, tall tales, and cartoons.

Some of Richard Serra's tapes also draw from commercial TV. *Television Delivers People,* 1974, for example, makes its ironic statements about the imperialism of commercial television in the seductive manner of advertisement. Messages such as "POPULAR ENTERTAINMENT IS BASICALLY PROPAGANDA FOR THE STATUS QUO," "Control over broadcasting is an exercise in controlling society," and "CORPORATIONS ARE NOT RESPONSIBLE" roll down a bright blue background to a zippy Muzak accompaniment. In this tape Serra criticizes the medium from within the medium itself. To have any political impact, however, the tape would need to be shown on a major TV network rather than in the art gallery or even on cable TV. *Match Match Their Courage,* 1974, was made in a television studio. It used a delayed audio-feedback system and a split screen which showed two performers, each of whom could see the other on a monitor only and could hear only the delayed sound of their voices as they were fed back through their earphones. Each performer's character was suggested by a color—one cool blue, the other warm orange. *Prisoner's Dilemma,* 1974, made with Robert Bell, was structured on a problem in game theory, a "non-zero sum game." The first half, modelled on the TV cops-and-robbers genre, used professional actors who turned the situation into TV theater by playing to the camera. The second half was like a TV quiz show, and was taped from a live performance in which contestants were goaded by an M.C. to respond extemporaneously for a reward or a punishment. The "punching," or rapid switching from one image to another, by Serra and Carlota Schoolman who controlled three cameras through the SEG board, was reminiscent of early TV situation comedy.

While these and other videotapes have found ways of dealing with video processes characteristic to the medium, they are still dependent upon the continuum of linear reading and the relation between the monitor and a relatively arbitrary external situation. Although the creation of certain effects in these tapes may be achieved through technologies particular to video, the viewer's experience of these effects is no different from the experience of analagous effects in other media. For example, an SEG allows a simultaneous presentation of several points of view, but the split screen on film also permits this, although less directly. One experiences an illustration or picture of simultaneity—a way of reading more elements into a whole, bounded conventionally by a frame—rather than actually experiencing simultaneous events. Video feedback is also understood at a remove, read back into the history of the tape rather than experienced directly.

In contrast to the video matrices, other closed-circuit video environments really have been able to engage the viewer in their modes of presentation. In these pieces, video is used as a medium for creating interaction between the viewers and the space they occupy. This interaction is possible because the artist's attention is focused on the visceral response of the viewer rather than on the mechanical workings of the video. The difference between these pieces and closed-circuit video matrices is that the latter are sculptures *in* an environment while the former *are* environments. These pieces resemble theater more than sculpture, and the actors and actresses are the viewers who participate in a drama inherent in the setting itself.

Bruce Nauman was the first artist to move video into the room. His Performance Corridors of 1969 and his closed-circuit systems use mirrors, video, light, and techniques such as masking part of the camera lens to create in the viewer feelings of displacement and disorientation. The mind's memory of the body is disturbed at its most basic level, as the self is recognized in several uncharacteristic appearances simultaneously, as the recurrent images are integrated into a single moment. For example, in *Video Surveillance,* 1969, a television camera was placed at the outside entrance and a monitor at the other end of a corridor thirty-five feet long and twenty-five inches wide. The viewer had to walk about ten feet into the corridor before appearing on the television screen. The camera had a wide-angle lens and was placed ten feet above the floor. Viewers saw themselves on the screen from the back and from above, totally unlike their usual experience of themselves. In a piece at the Reese Palley Gallery in San Francisco, the viewer created and moved within an invisible corridor by maintaining a certain distance from the monitor as set forth in the rules of the piece:

> The point of the piece is to make a visual corridor in which you must walk in order to keep yourself visible on the monitor screen. At the same time, one must keep oneself visible on the monitor in order to stay in the corridor. The problem is rendered more difficult because a) the camera does not point at the monitor so that walking toward the screen does not keep you in the picture, in fact leads you out of it; b) the cameras are rotated on their horizontal axis 90 degrees and 180 degrees so that the image on the monitor is either sideways or upside down; c) the camera which records the image on your reference screen is always at your back so that the image is always of your back.[17]

This dissociation in elementary body perception accounts for an apparently inexhaustible number of sensations:

> It had to do with going up the stairs in the dark, when you think there is one more step and you take the step, but you are already at the top...or going down the stairs and expecting there to be another step, but you are already

at the bottom. It seems that you always have that jolt and it really throws you off. I think that when these pieces work they do that too. Something happens that you didn't expect and it happens every time. You know why and what's going on but you just keep doing the same thing.[18]

These and other pieces by Nauman do operate at the process level of perception, as the transaction between viewer and environment is constantly regenerated.

Peter Campus's closed-circuit pieces also create the simultaneous experience of different modes of appearance in a space by the use of live, video, mirror, and shadow images which cause feelings of dissociation in the viewers who must experience something other than the familiar, integrated manifestations of themselves. Like Nauman, Campus understood that this experience of simultaneity could happen only in a video environment:

> In a closed circuit video situation one is no longer dealing with images of a temporally finite nature. The duration of the image becomes a property of the room.[19]

While cybernetic parallels between human perception and the machine have been claimed by artists working with video matrices, their technologies may provide metaphors for vision but they do not set up conditions in which visual processes occur. Campus has tried to create a dialogue between the viewer and the environment rather than to construct perceptual maps:

> If we are to avoid the problem of creating a visual system that will reduce the capacity of the eye, it is necessary to disassociate the video camera from the eye and make it an extension of the room....
>
> Instead of limiting the amount of visual information coming to the eye-brain by replacing the natural field of vision with an abstracted one, it is possible to include the video information in the viewer's field of vision, increasing the potential of the visual system....
>
> The video camera makes possible an exterior point of

view simultaneous to one's own. The advance over the film camera is due to the vidicon tube, similar to the retina of the eye, continuously transposing light (photon) energy to electrical energy.

The monitor is an object sitting rigidly in space. This allows the viewer to locate the monitor in space relative to him/her. Compare this to a movie theater where every effort is made to erase one's ability to locate the screen in the viewer's space, containing all possibilities for central (foveal) eye movements. In a video monitor situation, central eye movements tend to move off the surface of the screen, locating the screen and relating the screen to the room.[20]

Campus's pieces employ binary relationships such as light-dark, negative-positive, projected and reflected light, and present and past events in such a way that the viewer mediates between the mechanism of the video and the image it produces. As in Nauman's corridors, most of Campus's pieces (except for *Kiva*, 1971, a self-sustained system) require the viewer's presence for their realization: the viewer is the trigger as well as the material for the work. One must physically explore a piece to discover the coordinates of the field in which the piece exists visually. Within this area, the focus is on simultaneous and disconnected modes of appearance. For example:

> In *Shadow Projection* [1974]...a spotlight and a video projector stand on opposing sides of a translucent screen located 18 feet from each light source. Upon entering the brilliant white field created by the theatrical spotlight, a video camera located directly beneath the light picks up the viewer's well-lit image and transmits it by cable to the projector. The shadow created by the viewer standing between the light and the screen is filled in by the video projected image of the viewer thrown from the opposite side of the screen. As the viewer moves in the field, the properties of the inverse square law regulate the proportional size of the shadow to the video projection....What Campus sets up in this piece is a field in which the interplay and difference between the shadow image and the projected image becomes a property of the viewer's motion in the light-defined field....

In *Negative Crossing* [1974] the field is split into halves. On one side of a screen, a camera mounted on top of a picture monitor establishes a split screen, positive-negative situation. The negative image is superimposed over the positive if the viewer finds the mid-point in the field. A projector, located behind the screen, repeats the monitor image creating a situation in which the viewer is caught between the monitor camera and the projection....The sum total of the forces at play tends to lead the viewer into a centralized rotation in an effort to apprehend the work, and mediate between the opposing elements.

Stasis [1973] refers to calm in relation to motion. The viewer, upon entering the field of light and camera angle, is confronted with two views of him- or herself. One view is a stationary full-length shot, the other is a three-quarter length view that is rotated through a motorized revolving prism. Depending upon the viewer's position within the field the two images may either float away from each other (as if in some dream-like state) or, when centrally located, the viewer's image rotates (on an axis located in the stomach) around the stationary head of the static image.[21]

Some of the closed-circuit environments by Nauman have been among the most abstract works in video: given properties inherent in the medium, such as simultaneity through feedback, these pieces create their own conditions of presentation, independent of externally determining frameworks such as broadcasting or the monitor within an arbitrary display situation. In these works, form emerges as a convergence of content and structure. The other schools of video are unable to achieve greater abstraction because of economic limitations. Artists' tapes aired on broadcast television (such as "Video Visionaries" on WNET-TV in New York) are not sufficiently distinct from commercial programming to be dissociated from network imperialism and are subsumed in the megalithic system. Seen out of context and transposed to a framework of more sophisticated technology, these tapes seem to appease

the desire for something "avant garde" without posing any threat to the ruling corporations. Until an independent and equivalent structure for presentation is realized financially and politically, there will be no network TV by artists.

The conditions in which videotapes are shown in galleries also undercut their ability to create primary forms. Such work has the possibility of abstraction through modes of presentation—the intimacy of the close-up and of sound in a dialogue with the individual viewer—but most galleries and museums are not equipped to handle these requirements. Monitors are usually placed in spaces so large that the monitor is only a small object in a relatively large environment and the sound is diffused (or confused, if more than one tape is playing), eliminating any possibility of direct contact. Perhaps public display is antithetical to such work; it may be that only wide-scale private ownership will permit this intimacy.

These are some of the reasons why video still seems to be dependent upon forms outside of itself, whether from art or mass culture. Until it can create more independent structures of composition and presentation, video will continue to illustrate the processes it borrows.

FOOTNOTES

1. Nam June Paik, "Norbert Wiener and Marshall McLuhan," in *Nam June Paik: Video 'n' Videology,* ed. Judson Rosenbush (Syracuse, N.Y.: Everson Museum of Art, 1974), p. 28.

2. Jan van der Marck, "George Brecht: An Art of Multiple Implications," *Art in America* (July 1974):49.

3. Rosenbush, ed., *Nam June Paik,* p. 55.

4. Frank Gillette, in *Video: Process and Meta-process,* ed. Judson Rosenbush, essays by Frank Gillette and Willoughby Sharp (Syracuse, N.Y.: Everson Museum of Art, 1973), p. 27.

5. Ibid., p. 27.

6. John S. Margolies, "TV—the Next Medium," *Art in America* (September 1969):50.

7. Gene Youngblood, *Expanded Cinema,* foreword by R. Buckminister Fuller (New York: E.P. Dutton & Company, 1970), p. 343.

8. Margolies, "TV—the Next Medium," p. 49.

9. Jane Livingston and Marcia Tucker, *Bruce Nauman, Work from 1965 to 1972* (Los Angeles: Los Angeles Museum of Art, 1972), p. 3.

10. Lisa Bear, ed., "Bruce Nauman," an interview with Bruce Nauman, *Avalanche* (Winter 1971):25.

11. Livingston and Tucker, *Bruce Nauman,* p. 34.

12. Lisa Bear, "Keith Sonnier....New York—LA Hookups," an interview with Keith Sonnier, *Avalanche Newspaper* (May 1974):24-25.

13. Allan Kaprow, "Hello: Plan and Execution," *Art-Rite* (Autumn 1974):18.

14. Lisa Bear, ed., "Body As Place—Moving in on Myself, Performing Myself," *Avalanche* (Fall 1972):18.

15. Lisa Bear, "Vito Acconci....Command Performance, An Interview with Vito Acconci," *Avalanche Newspaper* (May 1974):22.

16. Idem.

17. Livingston and Tucker, *Bruce Nauman,* p. 28.

18. Bear, ed., "Bruce Nauman," p. 30.

19. Peter Campus, in *Peter Campus.* Essays by Peter Campus, James Harithas, and David A. Ross. (Syracuse, N.Y.: Everson Museum of Art, 1974), n.p.

20. Ibid., Peter Campus.

21. Ibid., David A. Ross.

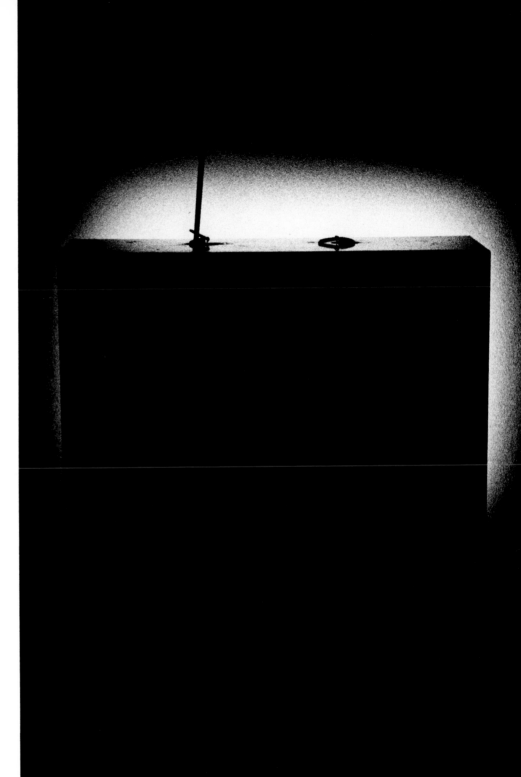

Douglas Davis   *Image from the Present Tense I*   1971

SACRAMENT AND TELEVISION
Jack Burnham

There is a small but growing clan of artists who are finding promise, if not salvation, through the medium of television. If one were to announce to a group of academic art historians that television is one of the inevitable and logical successors to a thousand years of the Western Art Tradition the statement would be greeted with incomprehension, benign amusement, or angry denial. Still, Television Art is here in galleries and in some museums. Its very presence tells us a good deal about the state of art. What is more, it gives us a glimpse of both the beginning and end of art as a cyclical phenomenon. As for the perennial problem of "quality" besetting High Art, video goes its own way and seems to be more interested in the day-to-day problems of acting effectively in various social contexts.

As a critic I am not particularly addicted to television as an art form; however, the literature of the medium really interests me. For instance in 1971 Michael Shamberg published a large paperback, *Guerrilla Television,* an outgrowth of his early support of the magazine *Radical Software.* In the last two years, Frank Gillette's *Between Paradigms: The Mood and its Purpose* appeared, as did *Cybernetics of the Sacred* by Paul Ryan. These books have in common a certain evangelical fervor concerning the possibilities of videotape as a medium of artistic and, more importantly, of communal expression and exploration. Looking back on what is disparagingly referred to as "Teck-Art"—that is, the kinetic sculpture and luminous art of the 1960s—Television Art displays enormously more sophistication in the financing of its technology, relationships with corporate structures, social ethics and application, and in the aesthetics of the work itself. Not surprisingly, there is a collective energy which has contributed a particular flavor to the writings of this group; Joycean hyperbole as used by

Paul Kos *REVOLUTION: Notes for the Invasion MAR MAR MARCH*   1972-1973

McLuhan is plentiful, as are the technical-verbal agglutinations so loved by Buckminster Fuller. Video prose is influenced by the writings of a handful of favorite philosophers, mystics, and poets, and interlarded with the hip language of Downtown New York. It sounds unreadable, and at times it is. Nevertheless a messianic call to a new age of communication shines through these writings.

Of the three, Shamberg's *Guerrilla Television* is the most literate and informative. He offers particularly keen insights into the morality of the individuals who control the medium. He talks about lending equipment to other users, dealing with large corporations, the abnormal self-consciousness of homemade video, and using video as a means of raising "grassroots consciousness." The theme that there is a large anonymous audience "out there" just waiting to turn TV against the exploiters of culture, makers of consumer goods, and particularly corporation-media itself is a favorite—because it is a direct extension of the essential concept of communication *feedback* as a form of social prophylaxis.

To my knowledge no other movement connected with the fine arts has given its literature quite such an apocalyptic tone, nor dwelled on the theme of history's obsolescence with the same enthusiasm; "The past is history and history is over"[1] is Gillette's encapsulation of the present. Paul Ryan, who studied several years for the priesthood, writes with similar enthusiasm in *Cybernetics of the Sacred.* For Ryan the task of the "sacred" is to perform an eternal balancing act between the natural ecology and man's attempts to deal with technology. To Ryan, ecology is akin to "God's House"—the harmonious interaction of every sphere of the Universe. Here television seems to be the binding medium which, if it has not exactly produced that

cliché of the 1960s, the "Global Village," it has at least united the artists and technicians who make up the Television Movement.

As with all art before it, television is a creature of illusion and, as in the past, the goddess of illusion seems always to stand "out there," just beyond the reach of corporal contact. Paradoxically, the alternate television movement in part beguiles the art audience by its kinship with the omnipotent powers of network television, so that some of the aura of network programming, with its fame and money, descends on the mundane figures of Television Art. The taboos of network television, however, are frequently broken by Television Art which uses deliberate repetition, private candor (on occasion), sexual explicitness, and downright monotony. Its little-boy misbehavior militates against the split-second solemnity of Big Brother, the networks.

The formats of Video Art may be described fairly simply. On the one hand, arrangement of the hardware is paramount. Multiple monitors with multiple channels programmed with the same materials presented from different camera angles and with contrasts of color and image-resolution, slow motion and superimposed images, etc. are all basic elements. On the other hand, Video Art evolves from Body Art, where the artist uses improvisations or set pieces to enact bits of drama, ritual, work, or intrapersonal encounters. While there is a strong bias among a number of artists toward formal arrangements in which the monitors themselves play a part in structuring the environment, televised Body Art mainly depends upon the editing of the videotapes themselves. On occasion, both forms can be and are integrated. The point is that, for the most part, Television Art relies upon the simplest "aesthetic" means possible—it shuns and leaves behind the formal devices and complexity of so-called High Art, and in its place desires an honest, easy give-and-take with the world around it. In ridding itself of High Art mannerism it seeks to become another communication loop with life at large.

Quite possibly it is this willingness of Television Art not merely to imitate life but to become one with it that gives its literature an apocalyptic flavor. There is the implication that television is the instrument which will transform an age of spiritual density, with its obtuse artistic pleasures, into the coming age of sacred revelation. The title of Frank Gillette's book, *Between Paradigms,* suggests that television is the interface between the modern myth of historical causality, what he terms "Amyth," and its diametrical opposite, an era of Nothingness which paradoxically provides us with Everything. Gilette insists, "We (our cultures, myths, systems) are traumatized by this unremitting interaction of the knowable and its passage to the *bete noire,* the void."[2] He is saying that we *are* what we *know,* and that our knowledge is about to take a quantum leap by virtue of an enormous extension of our being through television. The implication of Gillette's thesis is that art as we know it has a strange kind of built-in self-justification, while conversely, Television Art provides, through de-aestheticization, a life-model which incorporates all the mechanisms of feedback, which, in turn, constantly sustains us through humor, self-revelation, and heightened awareness—always on an "on-line," minute-to-minute basis.

Elsewhere Gillette states, "Ontological survival demands we revive our waning capacity to celebrate mystery, which remains our only experienced absolute."[3] Here is the key to sacramental celebration: constant revitalization through the reliving of the original mystery. Art must die, both constantly and periodically, so that life may be born, so as to give birth to art again. One is no less authentic than the other but, rather, art and life seem to be complementary, and thus inevitably locked together. As Gillette says: "As art is the successful communion of a variety, life's paradox is identical with art's: Affinities for opposites changing into one. In seeking the more perfect illusion, art seeks life."[4]

Without too much difficulty, it is easy to envision television as a kind of human eye attached to a purposeful brain. The electron beam scanning the phosphor on the inside of a video tube has all the ephemerality that we ordinarily associate with the ever shifting light falling on the mosaic of receptors in the human eye. Nothing lasts, and the medium, with all its flexibility, can and occasionally does become an extension of our own bodies—as Paul Ryan explains: "Wow, it's like making it with yourself."[5] Sexual excitement through self-admiration is evident not only in the prose of Television Art, but frequently in the tapes themselves. The blatant narcissism of Michelangelo's "Dying Slave" or Hans Belmer's dolls is reminiscent of a session in Gestalt therapy or an in-group joke when it is translated onto tapes. We begin to see that perhaps the original sin was self-consciousness and that our first images of God were in reality secret images of ourselves—but now it can be told, as they say, in living color. Yet if feedback through the ecologically minded use of television is a form of social therapy, are not these images on videotape just as destructive to true spontaneity and creativity as the miles and miles of masterpieces seen in museums?

In Post Formalist Art, particularly in television, the art act becomes subjective, immediate, and is constantly renewed, while the history of Western art can be read as a steady objectification of the archetypal acts called the holy sacraments. The replication and distribution of videotapes by the commercial gallery are becoming just as much legal business matters as the sale of paintings, prints, and sculptures ever was. However it is in the nature of art forms to have a foot in both worlds—to be made viable by the very mechanisms that ultimately stultify artists and lead them to acknowledge their spiritual and aesthetic inadequacy. Thus it is the *making* and not the repetitious *viewing* which lies at the heart of art, and this is the secret truth which no one must divulge for the fear that it would destroy our covetous attitude towards paintings and videotapes, which are, after all, merely objects.

Since I have intimated that all art is sacred, it might be well to look into the etymology of the words "sacred" and "sacrament." The word "sacrament" came into the language through Old French from the Latin word *sacramentum,* which meant a sworn obligation sanctioned by religious rite. Sacraments differ from the other rites of the Church in that they are channels through which supernatural grace is imparted; they are enacted outward and are the visible signs of inward grace. In Christian Latin from the third century, *sacramentum* was the accepted rendering for the Greek word for mystery, *mystērion,* meaning truths which are beyond the range of unassisted human apprehension; in essence, mystery is knowledge about the universe withheld. The word "sacrifice" also comes to mind as an extension of sacrament: sacrifice is the offering to a higher power, in basest terms the slaughter of an animal with its subsequent consumption by fire on the alter. Here we might look at *sacre* as being connected to the "s" sound in a derivation older than the Greek or Latin, that is, in the Chaldean or Hebrew letter *shin* which is the mother letter of FIRE. In a fundamental

way the sacred has to do with fire as the alchemical element responsible for the inordinate repetition of images, ultimately purging these images of their newness and "life" and thus leaving us with only the ashen residue of their spiritual meaning. We may look at art too as an extension of sacrament, and at sacrament historically as a progressive debasement of the archetypal religious acts, first reduced to icon, then to pictorial image, then to formal object, and finally to recorded activity itself. In every case, materiality, and the perception of it, are transformed in some degree to spirit. And it is the lived embodiment of sacrament which ultimately obviates art, and which is eventually consigned to FIRE.

In the secularity and crudeness of most Video Art there is an appeal to one of the oldest strictures concerning religious art, namely that the least pleasing and the least beautiful images of the gods (ourselves) tend to be the most holy. They tend to be closer to the core of mystery.

One of the main formal features of the art of the 1960s was a reliance on the repetition of trivial imagery. Manifest in the silkscreens of Warhol, the stripes of Buren, the "Disposables" of Levine, Antin's "Boots," and the multiple editions by many sculptors is the emotion of *ennui,* of weariness with "things," a fondness for multiplicity for its own sake. Multiple images symbolize the vacuousness of modern life and parallel the infinity of images generated by television as video approximates the stimulus-seeking rapaciousness of the human eye, with no rest or respite. Mircea Eliade's profound study of the nature of myth and symbolism in religion, *The Sacred and the Profane,* contains a powerful passage describing the transition from meaningful to meaningless repetition.

The perspective changes completely when the sense of *the religiousness of the cosmos becomes lost.* This is what occurs when, in certain more highly evolved societies, the intellectual elites progressively detach themselves from the patterns of the traditional religion. The periodical sanctification of cosmic time then proves useless and without meaning. The gods are no longer accessible through the cosmic rhythms. The religious meaning of the repetition of paradigmatic gestures is forgotten. But *repetition emptied of its religious content necessarily leads to a pessimistic vision of existence.* When it is no longer a vehicle for reintegrating a primordial situation, and hence for recovering the mysterious presence of the gods, that is, *when it is desacralized,* cyclic time becomes terrifying; it is seen as a circle forever turning on itself, repeating itself to infinity.[6]

In a society where life itself is sacramental there would be no room for images or "others," mystery would rest in our own will to ephemeralize the sullen and resistant images of day-to-day existence. Mind would be everywhere at once, and our attempts to prove, through duplication, its absence are a way of reminding us that *we too* think. In a large sense I am sure that the more thoughtful artists of video realize this instinctively. We have, for example, something close to that effect in Frank Gillette's statement: "Tele-vision is an advanced technology programming a formal exhaustion into its ambience."[7]

FOOTNOTES

1. Frank Gillette, *Between Paradigms: The Mood and its Purpose* (New York: Gordon and Breach Science Publishers, Inc., 1973), p. 6.

2. Ibid., p. 18.

3. Ibid., p. 17.

4. Ibid., p. 100.

5. Paul Ryan, *Cybernetics of the Sacred* (Garden City, New York: Anchor Press/Doubleday, 1974), p. 28.

6. Mircea Eliade, *The Sacred and the Profane* (New York: Harcourt, Brace & World, Inc., 1959), p. 107.

7. Gillette, *Between Paradigms,* p. 46.

Control room, installation at Institute of Contemporary Art, Philadelphia

THE FUTURE OF TELEVISION: SOME THEORETICAL CONSIDERATIONS
John McHale

I would like to emphasise initially that we cannot deal meaningfully with the future of television as an isolated development. Nor is it enough to concentrate unduly on the singular possibilities of the medium itself—as technical instrument or new art form—without attention to the larger theoretical considerations. Television is severally compounded of techniques of recording, processing and transmission of information, of entertainment, news and market offerings. It is a cultural medium which overlaps with and interpenetrates the wide spectrum of other media in the society.

The future of television lies within an ongoing revolution in information and communications capabilities. The latest and most critical aspect of this revolution in both information *and* communications technologies—and their ancillary software—is that these create what is virtually a new information environment.

We are no longer dealing with the separate strands of evolution within these technologies but with the ways in which their convergent interaction now constitutes an unprecedented change in our overall social and cultural environment. The core of this change lies with electronic reproduction, processing and transmission systems, one of whose prime characteristics is the extremely rapid, low-cost diffusion of sound, image and other symbolic messages—and the attendant capacity to store, process and interrelate many different types of information.

The initial convergence of these systems may be located at a point in the mid-1950s with the digital transmission of information by telephone line. Since then they have become more complexly interlinked and expanded, from the level of global satellite

Viewing room, installation at Institute of Contemporary Art, Philadelphia monitoring and communications to that of individually interactive modes. We are dealing, therefore, with a fusion of hardware and software which not only amplifies our capacities but which, by its functions as screen, channel and 'multiplexer', actually reshapes the information content and perception of society itself—in ways that our conventional wisdom may not be able to foresee, comprehend, or effectively control.

It can be said with some certainty that societies which become centrally dependent upon this new information and communications base will be as different from the industrial society which we have known for the past century or so as that society differs from all the agrarian pre-industrial societies which preceded it. The possible configurations of institutions, governance, individual and collective value systems of the emerging information society, however, are still open to conjecture. The extent to which we are already in the information society phase is exemplified by the Watergate affair, for example, in which the central dialogue was concerned with access to, and control of, information.

Though we have disavowed, somewhat, the emphasis on technical developments in television, it may be useful, at this point, to review some of these briefly for discussion. The general line of forecasted development runs through the more widespread use of picturephone with ancillary flatscreen wall TV, in the next decade, going towards holographic, three-dimensional video in the next fifteen to twenty years. Paralleling these main lines are further developments in more sophisticated, more miniaturised, personal and portable systems. These would include:

1) *At the individual level*, various types of interactive two-way modes for remote, plain language, graphic and aural, input and output linkages to large-scale information 'utilities' and computer networks. Operational prototypes for these exist in the ARPA network and others.

Where 'broadcast' TV is somewhat limited by the number of signals which can be sent without interference, the implementation of this expansion to interactive TV and other communications systems depends on the shift to coaxial cable and community antenna which can dramatically increase the number of channels available for the two-way interactive mode. Predicated on this shift is the ideal, or idealized, concept of the total home information and communications center which, in addition to providing entertainment either as consumer or producer would give direct access to a variety of services. For example, 'instant' library and information storage, access and retrieval, with 'on-line' news facsimile and electronic mail service; remote medical attention and counselling; decentralised education, shopping, banking—and even 'work', where many on-the-job functions could equally well be conducted at home. The overall services and functions can be elaborated as the imagination wills!

2) *At the level of the local, national, and international society*, many of the individualised services above, expanded to the enhancement of other professional, business, and government requirements at these different levels. With the successive launching and interlinkage of the communications satellite capabilities into interactive networks, the 'global village' will compact further into a closer resemblance to the old face-to-face community. It will be, however, a community in which the pace and 'tempo' of events and 'informational' awareness of events is much greater and much more highly interactive in their feedback relationships than at any other period.

Film, radio, and television broadcasting, if managed in conjunction with space satellites, telegraph and telephone cables, are not far from achieving instantaneous communication on a global scale....the mass media revolution (has) accelerated the tempo and direction of world history....This stupendous flood of messages could not fail to speed up the pace of history in Western Europe, and eventually in Asia, Africa, South America and Oceania. The media of communications were employed in ways that exploited the marginal advantage of a "sign." By definition, an instrument of communications is specialised to the use of signs, and signs mediate between the subjective events (the "symbols") of communicators. The signs are parsimonious of physical resources, rendering it feasible to cover vast distances by means of sound, sight or electromagnetic waves. The media rapidly reach the attention of distant persons and cue them to act more quickly than they otherwise would be able to do.[1]

3) *The generalised pattern* would be a considerable broadening of the spectrum of communications *modalities* e.g. from the one-to-one mode of the telephone, to the one-to-many mode of the book, radio and broadcast TV—towards many-to-many and many-to-one modalities of different kinds. The range of these technical possibilities suggests a strong trend towards more open, participatory, and 'democratic' uses of new video possibilities as they become available to larger numbers of people in a more directly interactive manner. Questioning whether this trend is implicit, or merely assumed, returns us to our more central discussion of the overall environment of the information society.

In considering the larger theoretical aspects of the information society, some of the underlying social implications may be noted as follows:

1) *Changes in the central resource base.* All other resources are dependent upon information and knowledge for their perception and use. As resources in themselves, information and knowledge are unique in not being lessened or reduced by wider sharing and increased use—rather they tend to gain in the process. In gaining access to, and control of, larger areas of the electromagnetic spectrum via information and communications technologies, society moves from its classically economic zero-sum position to a non-zero-sum game situation of which we know little.

2) *Changes in the nature of power,* e.g., from the older power base of control over physical *product* wealth to potential control over the *process* wealth of information and communications. A new 'property' class emerges, whose property is in their heads, i.e., those who are skilled in access to, and manipulation of the new processes. "Who *knows* what will become more important than who *has* what."[2]

Again, where older forms of power are converted into newer power sources:

> In a highly communicative world, access to the communications broadcast resource is equivalent to partially political power....the sale of TV time for political advantage is equivalent to a conversion of economic power into political power. Similarly, TV's insatiable appetite for visible dramatic news provides the mechanism whereby the demonstration—or staged riot—can convert political zeal and energy into political support by galvanising sympathies or inspiring fears and quiet.[3]

Another aspect of the increasingly swift diffusion of news and comment via television is the sharp decrease in the 'time cushion' between the occurrence of problems and issues and their entry into public dialogue. Policy and decision makers are increasingly placed in day-to-day crisis management with regard to issues in public view.

To some extent the policy process becomes more open as more interest groups may *potentially* seek to intervene, question and seek leverage to influence public affairs. The temptation here, however, is to think in terms of an increasingly homogeneous response by large, broadly informed, national and international audiences with possibilities of instant plebiscite or referendum, 'soapbox television', and video voting on crucial issues. The reverse may actually occur as more channels and more interactive means become available.

Though the audience for large TV events is enormous, e.g., up to 1.5 billion for some global programs, the so-called mass audience is already highly diversified. Media multiplication may indeed lead to more fragmented attitudes, more specialised interest groups and decreased concensus.

Whilst subscribing to fashionable terms such as participatory, widening of alternatives, options, choices, etc., we do need to remember that the increase of options and choices also entails increase in the repertoire of responses, increase in the range of value preferences and so on. Though initially expanding the 'sense of community', of common norms and purposes, it is equally possible that a greater variety of media alternatives etc. will also weaken individual identification with any community, as we know it, in favor of a more personally idiosyncratic, more selective and shifting range of allegiances to institutional structures.

In certain ways, this also suggests the emergence of divergent 'information communities' with an increasingly heterogeneous pattern of individual response. The polity, for example, may become more issue oriented but on a changing issue-to-issue basis and hence more difficult to mobilise on broad concensual patterns.

It may also be suggested that, due to economies of scale and development, information and communications could become more centrally controlled resources, especially where coupled with a political climate of high centralisation and increased surveillance. The counter influences towards this are, obviously, more diversity of accessible systems and more individuals skilled in organising and using the new media. The latter, however, may be limited in effect by their stratified class position.

3) *Impacts on the individual.* Many of the negatives in the information society have already been voiced—the use of communications to mold public opinion, increased surveillance and monitoring of personal data, the invasion of privacy in various forms, the dissonance and strains of over stimulation and information 'swamping', etc.

The positive aspects have been given less attention. The amplification of capacities could significantly enhance the power that individuals may exercise over their personal lives. This is already evident in the extension of the sensing, storage and processing range of individuals—where transportation technologies have extended physical mobility, information and communications have greatly extended individual 'psychic' mobility.

For example, the copying machine, allowing every writer to be his own publisher, already makes for an extraordinary flow of personalised information exchange. In combination with the telephone, terminal and other devices, such elements have already created new associational groupings which transcend conventional institutional barriers. Associated with this is the rise in 'underground' papers, journals, books, film, audio and video cassette exchanges which now constitute a wide spectrum of personalised information and communications networks. As the technical devices become more available to more people at less cost, they have tended to spur a new wave in cultural forms.

The more specifically cultural impacts of television, and associated mass media, require separate attention. The general tendency is to extrapolate the 'hardware' possibilities into the future—with insufficient regard to our assumptions about, and understanding of, television's cultural and symbolic functions even in the present.

So far, we have been dealing mainly with the instrumental and cognitive aspects of television rather than the affective. In considering the latter, we are really talking more about *the 'signals' which change us rather than through which we change our environment!* Human society is essentially more centrally dependent on its common symbol systems and their *affective* role in communications than on its physically *effective* and instrumental technologies. The flow of symbolic messages provides both its cohesion and its 'reality'.

> Communication is essentially a social process. Sharing does not mean simply passing something, some sign from one person to another, it implies also that this sign is mutually accepted, recognised and held in common ownership or use by each person.[4]

In the larger sense our present society, with its particular qualities of speed of change, interdependence, global diffusion of information and innovation is the latest phase of a massive and ongoing cultural evolution. World communications, particularly radio and TV, diffuse through and interpenetrate local cultural traditions, and provide more commonly shared cultural experiences in a manner which is unparalleled in human history. To a considerable extent the media *are* a common cultural environment sharing and transmuting human symbolic needs and their expression on a world scale. In providing a constant stream of moving, fleeting images of that world for our daily appraisal they are part of an emerging planetary culture—whose relation to, and comparison with, previous cultural forms may be somewhat uncertain.

In reiterating the commonalty and 'global sharing'[5] of sets of images and symbols, we should, however, qualify the term mass culture as applied most typically to television. Mass culture and 'mass society' are concepts which grew out of the dystopian vision of standardised cultural forms, and their widely shared sets of common values which were presumed to lead to a society of increasingly uniform life styles, aims and purposes. It was viewed as a 'low culture' society whose mass-produced products were intrinsically inferior to the 'high culture' forms which preceded it.

On the score of social uniformity and lack of variety, the more denotably standardised society was the agrarian peasant community with its limited repertoire of socio-cultural forms and possible life strategies. The mass-production phase of the industrial society actually provides a far greater variety of cultural forms and life styles. The shift to a post industrial information society portends an even greater diversity of social and cultural forms.

> The high-scale societies of the Western World are becoming increasingly heterogeneous. They are becoming increasingly differentiated, comprising thousands of minority groups, *each* joined around common interests, common value systems and shared stylistic preferences that differ from those of other groups. As the sheer volume of information and knowledge increases, as technological developments further expand the range of

options, and as awareness of the liberty to deviate and differentiate spreads, more variations are *possible.* Rising affluence or, even more, growing desire for at least subcultural identity induces groups to exploit these options and to invent new ones. We might almost say that irregular cultural permutations are becoming the rule.[6]

We have then few critical precedents with which to evaluate our *present* cultural milieu—let alone to conjecture about its future. Most of the physical facilities which render it possible have not previously existed, and their transformative capacities pose more fundamental questions regarding cultural and social values then we may hint at here.

This examination of the overall position of the mass media is important in considering the future of television. The general commitment of those critically concerned with that future is to perpetuate an evaluative scale derived from the fine arts—whose application to a medium such as television may be singularly inappropriate. The traditional canons of uniqueness, endurance over time, universality of appeal etc. can give little insightful guidance to the evaluation of a form in which such qualities are rarely present. Such evaluation is also often linked to conditions of social and moral judgment whose pertinence may even be suspect in the fine arts.

The moral criticism of television has been particularly specious in dwelling upon its consumer-oriented aspects, its apparent tendencies not only to corrupt the young but to degrade the emotional experience and aesthetic taste of the older. One apt quotation may suffice here:

> Going to the theater is a festive occasion, while seeing television at home becomes an everyday routine....We do not become part of an audience but remain alone even if we are a particle in an invisible mass audience. We are

not especially dressed as for an opera performance but, on the contrary, most television viewing is done in a state of highly informal dress. There is an utter disrespect for the play and its author, with the exception of rare performances. Nobody bothers about wilfully interrupting the show by eating, talking, telephoning and leaving the room, and nobody seems to be bothered much by interruptions for commercials. The lack of awe is a form of indifference and alienation from one's own emotion.[7]

The lack of formality, of awe and constraint, may seem somewhat salutary! We may note, however, the confusion between one kind of cultural experience and another and the implicit demand that they be treated as though in the same plane.

There is also a denial of the both/and quality of television (and other areas of mass media) in that one is not forced to choose between one experience or another but may flexibly shift from one to another—*and* read a book or talk on the telephone at the same time. A somewhat similar point has been made in relation to classical music, though with more invidious conclusions:

> *all* music can now be heard at any hour and as domestic background. Tape, radio, the phonograph, the cassette, will emit an unending stream of music, at any moment or circumstance of the day....It explains the prodigality of the baroque and of the pre-classical chamber ensemble in the L.P. catalogue. So much of this music was, in fact, conceived as *Tafelmusik* and aural tapestry around the busy room.[8]

When we turn to other critical stances within the media we may find them equally suspect as indicators of the future. One trend is the cultivation and encouragement of an avant-garde video art form whose implicit goal is to rescue the medium from 'the wasteland'. Admirable and interesting as this may be in terms of the quality of the work of individual artists who seek to use the obvious potential of television as an expression medium, much of its output so far has been somewhat conventional.

In all too many cases, the actual products tend to be mere animated versions of what has already been prefigured in abstract painting, kinetic sculpture, light shows and film. There seems to be two main directions, *one*—to exploit the range of *technical* effects either with the camera itself, or in 'direct video' without the camera but using the various possibilities of direct electronic input into the receiver (a kind of video Moog synthesiser effect), or distorting the broadcast signal through various means to produce video collage effects); *the other* is the 'kino-eye', or candid camera, approach of continuous or discrete monitoring of processes or human actions and their transmission 'as given', or in combination with the former technical transformations.

The potential is certainly there for enlarging the spectrum of aural and visual image and symbol manipulation and making it available to more direct interaction. This point is well made in the following computer oriented comment:

> Could the functions of TV and the computer be integrated into some *new* device so as to be most useful and helpful in man's intellectual development? One may envision a device which is like a TV in that it is capable of generating visual images of rich and wondrous variety as well as displaying symbolic forms, while it is also like a computer in that it invites active participation of the viewer by enabling him to enter into the generation and control of the information being displayed. Then, for the first time, man would have the ability to create visual images easily for communicating ideas that he hitherto had little or no facility for expression.[9]

One may repeat again that the quality and promise of such work depends on individual talents which should in no way be denigrated. The lack of rigor in internal criticism of such work, however, partakes of the 'Emperor's clothes' syndrome. Our larger theoretical question is its relevance within the context of the future of television. There is certainly a strong tendency to overvalue such experimental modes as being on a higher plane than ordinary programming.

What is particularly apparent in such overvaluation is a denial of the larger symbolic and ritualistic functions of both the manifest and latent 'content' of television— as even extending to the commercial break. This is one area in which our critical appreciation of the mass media has, in general, been rather weak, with, of course, some notable exceptions such as McLuhan and, earlier, Parker Tyler.

The latter's stance, though referring more specifically to film criticism rather than television, is still relevant:

> Devotees of both stage and novel who scorn movies as below the serious level—as standing in relation to true art somewhat as the circus does to the legitimate stage. But unfortunately these judges, unaware of the ritual importance of the screen, its baroque energy and protean symbolism, are unwarrantably summary, basically uneducated in the movie medium.[10]

We might argue that it is in this area that our primary concern with the future lies—with the role of television as one of the main channels which provides a rich profusion of symbolic images, usable configurations of experiential behavior, and social metaphors which enable people to adapt to and control the rapid frequency of changes in the human condition. The collective symbols of the society are to be found here rather than exclusively in the fine arts.

The constant re-creation and ritualistic repetition of such metaphoric images matches up to the requirements of a highly mobile and plastic environment in providing a stream of replaceable and expendable ikons of human experience. Secular by definition but mythopoetic in function, the video ikons afford both the recurrent stability and ritualised predictability of the standard format series and the changing topicality (and fantasy) of the 'specials', the news, and other shows.

One may also underline the ways in which the range of ikonic heroes is adaptable to, and identifiable within, a wide range of marginal and minority audiences for whom some specifiable trait may be important. For example, the fat man, the crippled, and the aged, as exemplified by Cannon, Ironside and—the geriatric as detective—Barnaby Jones, or the blind as in Longstreet. It is not without latent significance that the nonviolent hero of Kung Fu is a halfcaste with the singular name of Cain. Even Paladin has crossed the frontier into the early twentieth century as the aging Hec Ramsey— trading in his travelling gun for a microscope and a Holmesian preoccupation with forensic science.

As I view it, then, one of the main problems in discussing the future of television lies with the critical viewpoint, i.e., as posing a dichotomy between TV as medium for high art or as "banal wasteland" of supposed mass culture. We have no overarching theory of aesthetics or cultural values which embraces both ends of what is essentially a fluid continuum rather than a polarised dichotomy. One need not seek for some internal consistency within such a theory— which might try, for example, to equate the intimate creative gesture of a brush drawing with the collective satellite broadcast of a Presley spectacular— on some monotone hierarchical scale. The former is part of, and expresses, the private dimension of experience, the latter of the public environment—

the significantly common element is that appreciation of the one does not preclude participation in the other.

At best, such a theory or aesthetic need only be descriptive and inclusive rather than hierarchical and exclusive. Its beginning formulation may be found in the early discussions surrounding the origins of pop art which extended aesthetic meaning and significance to the everyday objects and processes of contemporary living.

In terms of the future of art or the future of television, or indeed the future of culture, we are patently moving towards the cafeteria style of a cultural smorgasbord rather than the formal stages of an eight course dinner! It is no longer a question of *either/or* but of *both/and*— as a vastly enlarged range of experience becomes available according to personal taste and desire.

To an increasing extent, the future in general is potentially more open to our individual and collective choices and options than ever before, rather than being determined by externally constraining agencies. The role which television may play in molding that future is best served by enlarging rather than restricting the potential for both individual and collective participation in its interactive use. Our task is to evaluate the policies, and preferred directions, which may aid its role in broadening the imaginative reach and behavioral repertoire of human possibilities.

FOOTNOTES

1. Harold D. Lasswell, "The Future of World Communications: Quality and Style of Life" (Paper delivered at East-West Communications Institute, Honolulu, Hawaii, September 1972), p. 10.

2. Nicholas Henry, "The Future As Information," *FUTURES* Vol. 5, No. 4 (August 1964): 397.

3. Ben H. Badikian, *The Information Machines, Their Impact on Men and Media* (New York: Harper and Row, 1971), p. 249.

4. Golin Cherry, *World Communication: Threat or Promise* (London: Wiley-Interscience, 1971), p. 2.

5. The 'common sharing' aspect might also be qualified. As used to define the supposed coherence of the youth culture deriving from a common identity of symbols and meanings carried in pop music, it neglects the range and diversity of such music itself *and* its diverse audiences. A recent study suggests, indeed, that, "Although pop has undoubtedly extended the range of expressive styles open to adolescents, we would argue that their underlying values and definitions continue to come from class-based systems, rather than from pop....rather than creating a classless society of the young, pop is reaffirming class divisions..." Graham Murdock and Robin McCron, "Scoobies, Skins and Contemporary Pop," *New Society* Vol. 23, No. 547 (29 March 1973): 692.

6. Horst W. J. Rittel and Melvin M. Webber, "Dilemmas in a General Theory of Planning," *Policy Sciences* Vol. 4, No. 2 (June 1973): 167.

7. Marlin Grotjakn, M.D., *The Voice of the Symbol* (New York: Delta Books, 1973), p. 8.

8. George Steiner, *In Bluebeard's Castle: Some Notes towards the Re-definition of Culture* (London: Faber and Faber, 1971), p. 92.

9. William H. Huggins, "Iconic Communications," *IEEE Transactions on Education*, Vol. E-14, No. 4 (November 1971): 160.

10. Parker Tyler, *Magic and Myth of the Movies* (New York: Simon and Schuster, 1970), pp. xvii-xviii.

SELECTED BIBLIOGRAPHY

Books

Adler, Richard and Bau, Walter S., eds. *The Electronic Box. Office, Humanities and Arts on the Cable.* Essays by Robert R. Bruce, John Goberman, Kas Kalba, and others. New York: Praeger Publishers, 1974.

Barnouw, Erik. *A Tower in Babel: A History of Broadcasting in the United States.* Vol. I (to 1933). New York: Oxford University Press, 1966.

_____. *The Golden Web: A History of Broadcasting in the United States.* Vol. II (1933 to 1953). New York: Oxford University Press, 1968.

_____. *The Image Empire: A History of Broadcasting in the United States.* Vol. III (from 1953). New York: Oxford University Press, 1970.

Birdwhistell, Ray L. *Kinesics and Context: Essays on Body Motion Communication.* Philadelphia: University of Pennsylvania Press, 1970.

Bogart, Leo. *The Age of Television.* New York: Frederick Ungar Publishing Co., 1956.

Cage, John. *A Year from Monday: New Lectures and Writings by John Cage.* Middletown, Conn.: Wesleyan University Press, 1963.

Calas, Nicholas and Calas, Elena. *Icons and Images of the Sixties.* New York: E. P. Dutton & Co., 1971.

Carpenter, Edmund. *Oh, What a Blow That Phantom Gave Me!* New York: Holt, Rinehart & Winston, 1972.

Davis, Douglas. *Art and the Future.* New York: Praeger Publishers, 1973.

Nam June Paik *TV Garden* 1974

Fuller, R. Buckminster. *Nine Chairs to the Moon.* 1938. Reprint, Carbondale, Ill.: Southern University Press, 1963.

Gillette, Frank. *Between Paradigms: The Mood and Its Purpose.* New York: Gordon and Breach, 1973.

Goffman, Erving. *Interaction Ritual: Essays on Face to-Face Behavior.* Garden City, N.Y.: Anchor Books, 1967.

Johnson, Nicholas. *How to Talk Back to Your Television Set.* Boston: Little, Brown & Company, 1967.

Kosinski, Jerzy. *Being There.* New York: Harcourt, Brace, Javanovich, 1974.

Kulturman, Udo. *Art and Life.* Translated by John William Gabriel. New York: Praeger Publishers, 1971.

Laytourne, Kit, ed. *Doing the Media: A Portfolio of Activities and Resources.* New York: Center for Understanding Media, 1972.

McHale, John. *The Future of the Future.* New York: George Braziller, 1969.

McLuhan, Marshall. *Understanding Media: The Extensions of Man.* Boston: McGraw Hill, 1964.

Müller, Gregoire. *The New Avant Garde: Issues for the Art of the Seventies.* New York: Praeger Publishers, 1972.

Reichardt, Jasia, ed. *Cyberntic Serendipity: The Computer and the Arts.* Essays by Karlheinz Stockhausen, Norbert Wiener, and others. London: W & J Mackey & Co., 1968.

Rosenberg, Bernard and White, David Manning, eds. *Mass Culture Revisited.* New York: Van Nostrand Reinhold Co., 1971.

Ryan, Paul. *Cybernetics of the Sacred.* Garden City, N.Y.: Anchor Press/Doubleday, 1974.

Siepmann, Charles A. *Radio, Television and Society.* New York: Oxford University Press, 1950.

Shamberg, Michael and Raindance Corporation. *Guerilla Television.* New York: Holt, Rinehart, and Winston, 1971.

Smith, Ralph Lee. *The Wired Nation Cable TV: The Electronic Communications Highway.* New York: Harper & Row, 1972.

Stasheff, Edward and Bretz, Rudy. *The Television Program; Its Writing, Direction and Production.* New York: A. A. Wyn, 1951.

Teilhard de Chardin, Pierre. *The Pheonmenon of Man.* Translated by Bernard Wall. New York: Harper & Row, 1959.

TVTV. *The Prime Time Survey.* San Francisco: TVTV, 1974.

Wiener, Norbert. *Cybernetics: Or Control and Communication in the Animal and the Machine.* New York: John Wiley and Sons, 1948.

Youngblood, Gene. *Expanded Cinema.* New York: E. P. Dutton & Co., 1970.

Exhibition Catalogues

Nam June Paik: Electronic Art. Essay by John Cage. New York: Galeria Bonino, 1965.

Nam June Paik: Electronic Art II. Essay by Allan Kaprow. New York: Galeria Bonino, 1968.

Gerry Schum and Ursula Schum-Wever, eds. *Land Art.* Berlin: Fernsehgalerie Gerry Schum, 1969.

Kynaston L. McShine, ed. *Information.* Statements by the artists. New York: Museum of Modern Art, 1970.

Vision and Television. Foreword by Russell Connor. Waltham, Mass.: Rose Art Museum, Brandeis University, 1970.

Paik-Abe Video Synthesizer with Charlotte Moorman: Electronic Art III. Essays by John Cage and Russell Connor. New York: Galeria Bonino, 1971.

Circuit: A Video Invitational. Syracuse, N.Y.: Everson Museum of Art, 1972.

Douglas Davis: Events Drawings Objects Videotapes. Essays by James Harithas, Nam June Paik and David A. Ross. Syracuse, N.Y.: Everson Museum of Art, 1972.

Jane Livingston and Marcia Tucker. *Bruce Nauman, Work from 1965 to 1972.* Los Angeles: Los Angeles County Museum of Art, 1972.

Work from the Experimental Television Center, Binghamton, New York. Essay by David A. Ross. Syracuse, N.Y.: Everson Museum of Art, 1972.

Canada Trajectories 73. Introduction by Suzanne Pagé, essay on video by Werner Allen and statements by the artists. Paris: Musée d'Art Moderne de la Ville de Paris, 1973.

Judson Rosenbush, ed. *Frank Gillette Video: Process and Metaprocess.* Essay by Frank Gillette, interview by Willoughby Sharp. Syracuse, N.Y.: Everson Museum of Art, 1973.

Terry Fox. Essay by Brenda Richardson. Berkeley, Calif.: University Art Museum, Berkeley, 1973.

Trigon '73: Audiovisuelle Botschaften. Essays by Umbro Apollonio, Gillo Dorfles and Vera Horvat-Pintaric. Graz, Austria: Neue Galerie am Landesmuseum Joanneum.

Video Art, Estetica Televisual. Essay by Neil Hickey. Chapultepec, Mexico: Museo de Arte Moderno en Chapaltepec, 1973.

Video Circuits. Essay by Eric Cameron. Guelph, Ontario: University of Guelph, McLaughlin Library, 1973.

Video. Rotterdam: Rotterdamse Kunststichting, 1973.

William Wegman. Introduction by Jane Livingston. Los Angeles: Los Angeles County Museum of Art, 1973.

Americans in Florence: Europeans in Florence. Videotapes Produced by Art/Tapes/22. An exhibition at the Long Beach Museum of Art, Long Beach, California. Notes on the exhibition by David A. Ross. Florence: Centro Di, 1974.

Art Now 74, A Celebration of the American Arts. Essays by Richard Henshaw, David Ross, Jaromir Stephany, Nina Sundell and statements by the artists. Washington, D.C.: John F. Kennedy Center for the Performing Arts, 1974.

Art Video Confrontation 74. Essays by Dominique Belloir, Suzanne Pagé, Yann Pavie and others. Paris: Musée d'Art Moderne de la Ville de Paris, 1974.

Dennis Oppenheim. Statements by the artist. Amsterdam: Stedelijk Museum, 1974.

Mildred S. Friedman, ed. *New Learning Spaces and Places.* Catalogue to the exhibition held at the Walker Art Center. 90/91 *Design Quarterly* 1974.

Horst Gerhard Haberl. *Art As Living Ritual.* Graz: Pool der Poolerie, 1974.

Wulf Herzogenrath, ed. *Videotapes.* Cologne: Kölnischer Kunstverein, 1974.

Impact Art/Video Art 74. Essays by René Berger, Jole De Sanna and Luciano Giaccari. Lausanne: Galerie Impact, 1974.

Kunst bliebt Kunst, Catalogue Documentation for Projekt '74, Köln. Essays on video by Wulf Herzogenrath and David A. Ross. Cologne: Wallraf-Richartz-Museum, 1974.

Peter Campus. Essays by Peter Campus, James Harithas and David A. Ross. Syracuse, N.Y.: Everson Museum of Art, 1974.

Projected Images. Essays by Regina Cornwell, Nina Felshin, Martin Friedman, Annette Michelson, Robert Pincus-Witten, Barbara Rose and Roberta P. Smith. Minneapolis: Walker Art Center, 1974.

Judson Rosebush, ed. *Nam June Paik: Videa 'n' Videology 1959-1973.* Syracuse, N.Y.: Everson Museum of Art, 1974.

Video As an Art Form. Northampton, Mass.: Smith College Museum of Art, 1974.

Videoscape, An Exhibition of Video Art. Essays by Peggy Gale and Gary Neill Kennedy. Toronto: Art Gallery of Ontario, 1974.

Periodicals

Raffaele, Joe. "Nauman" in Joe Raffaele and Elizabeth Baker, "The Way-Out West: Interviews with San Francisco Artists." *Art News*, Summer 1967, p. 40.

Davis, Douglas. "Art & Technology—The New Combine." *Art in America*, January 1968, pp. 28-37.

Ryan, Paul. "The Raw and the Overcooked." *Media and Methods*, October 1969, pp. 48-50.

Ryan, Paul. "Videotape—Thinking about a Medium." *Media and Methods*, December 1968, pp. 36-41.

Yalkut, Jud. "Art and Technology of Nam June Paik." *Arts Magazine*, April 1968, pp. 50-51.

Levine, Les. "For Immediate Release." *Art and Artists*, May 1969, pp. 46-51.

Margolies, John S. "TV—The Next Medium." *Art in America*, September 1969, pp. 48-55.

Ryan, Paul. "Videotape and Special Education." *Audiovisual Instruction*, November 1969, p. 30.

Yalkut, Jud. "TV As a Creative Medium at Howard Wise Gallery." *Arts Magazine*, September 1969, p. 18.

Madsen, Alex. "The Third Revolution." *Sight and Sound*, Winter 1970, pp. 38-39.

Pincus-Witten, Robert. "Keith Sonnier: Exhibition at Castelli Warehouse." *Artforum*, May 1970, p. 75.

Plagens, Peter. "Keith Sonnier: Exhibition at Ace Gallery." *Artforum*, October 1970, pp. 85-88.

Sharp, Willoughby. "Nauman Interview." *Arts Magazine*, March 1970, pp. 22-27.

Smiley, Logan. "TV Film/Tape in the '70s." *Print*, January 1970, pp. 76-77.

Smiley, Logan. "TV: The Coming Cassette Revolution." *Print*, September 1970, pp. 70-76.

Stankiewicz, Karl. "Computer schreibt Bildmusik (Fachtagung in München: Fernsehen entwickelt neue Kunstformen)." *Kunstwerk*, February 1970, p. 43.

Tucker, Marcia. "PheNAUMANology." *Artforum*, September 1970, pp. 38-43.

Young, Joseph E. "Los Angeles, Bruce Nauman Exhibition at the Nicholas Wilder Gallery." *Art International*, Summer 1970, pp. 111-15.

Aaron, Chloe. "The Video Underground." *Art in America*, May 1971, pp. 74-79.

Baker, Kenneth. "Keith Sonnier at the Modern." *Artforum*, October 1971, pp. 77-81.

Blotkamp, Carel. "Dutch Artists on Television." *Studio International*, June 1971, pp. 276-77.

Bourdon, David. "Warhol As Filmmaker." *Art in America*, May 1971, pp. 48-53.

dell'Arco, Maurizio Fagiolo. "Lettera da Roma, Art Video Recording." *Art International*, October 1971, p. 38.

Goldberg, Mike. "Dear Editor: Many artists have found in small format videotape a new medium for creative expression." *Artscanada*, October 1971, p. 71.

Greenspun, Roger. "Film: Videotape Program at Whitney." *New York Times*, December 10, 1971.

Harrison, Charles. "Art on TV." *Studio International*, January 1971, pp. 30-31.

Jappe, George. "Projection: The New Trend at Prospect 71." *Studio International*, December 1971, pp. 258-61.

Jürgen-Fischer, Klaus. "Identifikationen: Gerry Schums zweite fernsehschau." *Kunstwerk*, January 1971, p. 47.

Morrissey, Paul and Hill, Derek. "Andy Warhol As a Filmmaker: A Discussion Between Paul Morrissey and Derek Hill." *Studio International*, February 1971, pp. 57-61.

Stoney, George C. "Mirror Machine [videotape and cable TV]." *Sight and Sound*, Winter 1971-72, pp. 9-11.

Tarshis, Jerome. "San Francisco." *Artforum*, February 1971, pp. 85-87.

Terbell, Melinda. "Los Angeles." *Arts Magazine*, April 1971, p. 74.

Trini, Tomaso. "Di videotape in videotappa [note sui primi esperimenti televisivi da parte degli artisti]." *Domus*, February 1971, pp. 49-51.

Trini, Tomaso. "Roma, VideObelisco." *Domus*, June 1971, p. 56.

Whitney, John H. "A Computer Art for the Video Picture Wall." *Art International*, September 1971, pp. 35-36.

Baert, Renée. "Video Recycled." *Artscanada*, October 1972, pp. 55-56.

Battcock, Gregory. "The Greening of Televideo and the Aesthetics of Boeing." *Domus*, April 1972, pp. 50-53.

Becker, Wolfgang. "Manhatten Ende 1971." *Kunstwerk*, March 1972, p. 15.

Davis, Douglas. "Video Obscura." *Artforum*, April 1972, pp. 64-71.

Dawson, Jan. "Other Channel." *Sight and Sound*, Autumn 1972, pp. 204-5.

Graham, Dan. "Eight pieces by Dan Graham 1966-72." *Studio International*, May 1972, pp. 210-13.

Hinshaw, Mark L. "Making the Medium Accessible." *Architectural Design*, November 1972, pp. 668-69.

Jardine, Bob and Hickie, Mike. "Some Ideas about Video and Community TV." *Architectural Design*, November 1972, pp. 669-70.

Lewis, Peter M. "Video." *Architectural Design*, May 1972, pp. 305-7.

Pincus-Witten, Robert. "Keith Sonnier: Video and Film As Color-field." *Artforum*, May 1972, pp. 35-37.

Reinke, Klaus U. "Video Artists." *Studio International*, February 1972, pp. 85-86.

Sloane, Patricia. "Video Revolution, Patricia Sloane Discusses the Work of Nam June Paik." *Art and Artists*, March 1972, pp. 28-31.

"Video News." *Architectural Design*, January 1972, pp. 9-10.

Altshuler, Jeffrey. "Film/TV: Electronic Editing." *Print*, July 1973, pp. 71-73.

Battcock, Gregory. "Explorations in Video." *Art and Artists*, February 1973, pp. 22-27.

Bear, Liza. "Man Ray Do You Want to . . ., "An interview with William Wegman. *Avalanche*, Winter/Spring 1973, pp. 40-51.

Boice, Bruce. "Lynda Benglis at Paula Cooper Gallery." *Artforum*, May 1973, p. 83.

Borgeaud, Bernard. "Cinéma et Video." *XXe Siècle,* December 1973, pp. 152-55.

Brook, Donald. "Idea Demonstrations: Body Art and 'Video Freaks' in Sydney." *Studio International,* June 1973, pp. 269-73.

Brooks, Rosetta. "Identifications at the Hayward Gallery." *Studio International,* April 1973, p. 197.

Connor, Russell. "A is for Art, C is for Cable." *American Film Institute Quarterly,* Fall 1973, pp. 19-23.

de Jong, Constance. "Joan Jonas: Organic Honey is Vertical Roll." *Arts Magazine,* March 1973, pp. 27-29.

Jappe, George. "Gerry Schum." *Studio International,* May 1973, pp. 236-37.

Katzive, David. "Museums Enter the Video Generation." *Museum News,* January 1973, pp. 20-24.

Kaufman, Michael T. "When Festival Is 10, Is It Avant-Garde." *New York Times,* December 10, 1973.

Kurtz, Bruce. "Fields: Peter Campus." *Arts Magazine,* May 1973, pp. 25-29.

Kurtz, Bruce. "Video Is Being Invented." *Arts Magazine,* December 1973, pp. 37-44.

Madsen, Axel. "Video." *Sight and Sound,* Summer 1973, p. 146.

Morris, Robert. "Exchange '73: From a Videotape by Robert Morris." *Avalanche,* Summer/Fall 1973, pp. 22-25.

Perreault, John. "Para-Television Daydreams." *Village Voice,* October 11, 1973, p. 37.

Reveaux, Anthony. "New Technologies for the Demystification of Cinema." *Film Quarterly,* Fall 1973, pp. 42-51.

Smith, Roberta. "Peter Campus at Bykert Gallery." *Artforum,* December 1973, pp. 81-82.

Trini, Tomaso. "Dan Graham, I/Eye." *Domus,* February 1973, p. 51.

Alliata, Vicky. "Videoconferenza al MOMA." *Domus,* April 1974, p. 55.

Brooks, Rosetta. "The Artists' Use of Video." *Flashart,* December 1973 - January 1974, pp. 9-10.

Cameron, Eric. "Videotape and the University Art Programme." *Studio International,* June 1974, pp. 289-91.

Carroll, Noel. "Joan Jonas: Making the Image Visible." *Artforum,* April 1974, pp. 52-53.

Collins, James. "Hannah Wilke at Ronald Feldman Gallery." *Artforum,* June 1974, pp. 71-72.

Cornwell, Regina. "XII Bienal de São Paulo: A Prototype for Vaudville." *Studio International,* March 1974, pp. 98-101.

Davis, Douglas. Letter. *Artforum,* November 1974, p. 8.

Davis, Douglas. "Public Art: The Taming of the Vision." *Art in America,* June 1974, pp. 84-85.

Frampton, Hollis. "The Withering Away of the State of Art." *Artforum*, December 1974, pp. 50-55.

Gillette, Frank. "Difference and Resemblance: Precis for Track/Trace, A Video Work by Frank Gillette." *Design Quarterly*, January 1974, pp. 33-34.

Hoffman, Judy; Olliger, Lilly; Korsts, Anda. "Chicago Women's Video Festival." *Women and Film*, 1974, no. I, pp. 107-8.

Kaprow, Allan. Letter. *Artforum*, November 1974, p. 8.

Kaprow, Allan. "Video Art: Old Wine, New Bottle." *Artforum*, June 1974, pp. 46-49.

Michishita, Kyoko. "Tokyo—New York Video Express." *Women and Film*, 1974, no. I, pp. 86-97.

Minton, James. "Melchert and Glassman." *Artweek*, February 9, 1974, pp. 1,14.

Moore, Alan. "Dennis Oppenheim at 112 Greene Street." *Artforum*, April 1974, pp. 81-82.

Moore, Alan. "Peter Campus, Andy Mann, Ira Schneider, Tom Marioni at The Everson Museum of Art." *Artforum*, June 1974, pp. 77-78.

O'Connor, John J. "TV: Meditating on Young Guru and His Followers, Maharaji Ji Is Focus of P.B.S. Documentary." *New York Times*, February 25, 1974.

Pincus-Witten, Robert. "Nam June Paik at the Bonino Gallery." *Artforum*, April 1974, p. 70.

Pincus-Witten, Robert. "Open Circuits: The Future of Television." *Artforum*, April 1974, p. 70.

Smith, Roberta. "Doug Davis at Fischbach Gallery." *Artforum*, June 1974, pp. 73-74.

Smith, Roberta. "William Wegman Exhibition at Sonnabend Gallery; Dennis Oppenheim Exhibition at John Gibson Gallery." *Artforum*, May 1974, pp. 70-1.

Sullivan, Pat. "The 2nd Annual Women's Video Festival." *Women and Film*, 1974, p. 96.

Weibel, Peter. "Zur Philosophie von VT & VTR." *Heute Kunst*, December 1973 - February 1974, pp. 13-15.

Lorber, Richard. "Epistemological TV." *Art Journal*, Winter 1974/75, pp. 132-34.

Periodicals About Video

Art and Cinema. New York: Visual Resources, Inc.

Bulletin for Film and Video Information. New York: Anthology Film Archives.

Film Video Extra. London: Greater London Arts Association.

Mass Media Booknotes. Philadelphia: Department of Radio-Television-Film, Temple University.

Radical Software. New York: Gordon and Breach.

Radio Electronics. New York: Gernsbach Publications.

The Television Laboratory News. New York: The Television Laboratory, WNET/13 division of The Educational Broadcasting Corporation.

Televisions. Washington, D. C.: Washington Community Video Center.

TV Guide. Radnor, Pa.: Triangle Publications, Inc.

Video Info, Le Journal de la video. Paris: Collectif Video.

The Video Publisher. White Plains, N. Y.: Knowledge Industry Publications.

Special Issues About Video

Print, January 1972. Robert de Havilland, guest editor. Contributions by Fred Barzyk, Sheldon Satin, Michael Shamberg, and others.

Artscanada, October 1973. Contributions by Robert Arn, Fujiko Nakaya, Carol Zemel, and others.

Avalanche Newspaper, May 1974. Contributions by Joseph Beuys, Ulrike Rosenbach and William Wegman, and interviews with Vito Acconci, Chris Burden, Keith Sonnier, and others.

Art-Rite, Autumn 1974. Anna Canepa, guest editor. Contributions by artists.

Arts Magazine, December 1974. Contributions by Russell Connor, Dan Graham, David Ross, and others.

Catalogues of Videotapes

Artists Videotapes from Electronic Arts Intermix. New York: Electronic Arts Intermix, 1975.

Castelli-Sonnabend Videotapes and Films. Tape descriptions by Lizzie Borden and Nina Sundell. New York: Castelli-Sonnabend Tapes and Films, 1974.

Video Exchange Directory 3. Vancouver, B.C.: The Satellite Video Exchange Society, 1974.

The Video Distribution, Inc. New York: The Video Distribution, Inc, 1974.

INSTITUTE
OF
CONTEMPORARY
ART